MOTHERS HAVE

# Angel Wings

## A TRIBUTE TO THE TEARS AND
## TRIUMPHS OF BEING A MOM

Compiled and Edited by

# Carol Kent

**NAVPRESS** ◑
BRINGING TRUTH TO LIFE
P.O. Box 35001, Colorado Springs, Colorado 80935

## OUR GUARANTEE TO YOU

We believe so strongly in the message of our books that we are making this quality guarantee to you. If for any reason you are disappointed with the content of this book, return the title page to us with your name and address and we will refund to you the list price of the book. To help us serve you better, please briefly describe why you were disappointed. Mail your refund request to: NavPress, P.O. Box 35002, Colorado Springs, CO 80935.

The Navigators is an international Christian organization. Our mission is to reach, disciple, and equip people to know Christ and to make Him known through successive generations. We envision multitudes of diverse people in the United States and every other nation who have a passionate love for Christ, live a lifestyle of sharing Christ's love, and multiply spiritual laborers among those without Christ.

NavPress is the publishing ministry of The Navigators. NavPress publications help believers learn biblical truth and apply what they learn to their lives and ministries. Our mission is to stimulate spiritual formation among our readers.

Library of Congress Catalog Card Number: 96-51870
ISBN 1-57683-001-2

Cover illustration: © 1995 Anthony D' Agostino

Most of the anecdotal illustrations in this book are true to life and are included with the permission of the persons involved. All other illustrations are composites of real situations, and any resemblance to people living or dead is coincidental.

Unless otherwise identified, all Scripture quotations in this publication are taken from the HOLY BIBLE: NEW INTERNATIONAL VERSION ® (NIV®). Copyright © 1973, 1978, 1984 by International Bible Society. Used by permission of Zondervan Publishing House. All rights reserved. Other versions used include: The New American Standard Bible (NASB), © The Lockman Foundation 1960, 1962, 1963, 1968, 1971, 1972, 1973, 1975, 1977; The Message: New Testament with Psalms and Proverbs (MSG) by Eugene H. Peterson, copyright © 1993, 1994, 1995, used by permission of NavPress Publishing Group; Scripture quotations marked (NLT) are taken from the Holy Bible, New Living Translation, copyright © 1996. Used by permission of Tyndale House Publishers, Inc., Wheaton, Illinois 60189. All rights reserved. Scriptures quoted from The Holy Bible, New Century Version (NCV), copyright © 1987, 1988, 1991 by Word Publishing, Dallas, Texas 75039. Used by permission.

Mothers have angel wings : a tribute to the tears and triumphs of being a mom / compiled and
    edited by Carol Kent.
        p.    cm.
    ISBN 1-57683-001-2 (pbk.)
    1. Mothers—Religious life.  2. Mother and child—Religious aspects—Christianity.  I.
Kent, Carol, 1947–     .
BV4847.M68     11997
242'.6431—dc21                                                                    96-51870
                                                                                      CIP

Printed in the United States of America

5 6 7 8 9 10 11 12 13 14 15 16 17 18 / 05 04 03 02

FOR A FREE CATALOG OF
NAVPRESS BOOKS & BIBLE STUDIES,
CALL 1-800-366-7788 (USA)
or 1-416-499-4615 (CANADA)

# Contents

This Book is Lovingly Dedicated
To the Dearest Mother in the World

Pauline Wielhouwer Afman

You prayed for me before I was born.
You led me to Jesus when I was five years old.
You told me I was beautiful when a boy
    in fourth grade said I had big lips.
You dramatized stories in such an exciting way
    that I fell in love with spoken and written
    words.
You encouraged me to get an education and to
    invest my life in things that last forever.
You covered me with prayer and supported
    my dreams.

And now, as I'm watching you sit in the hospital
    day after day as Daddy struggles for every
breath, you are teaching me how to develop an
    eternal perspective.

I can never repay you for your investment in my life,
    but I can pass on the things you have taught me
    to the next generation.

I love you, Mama.

# *Acknowledgments*

Writing a book is a lot like building a house. While this project came together, I was in the process of moving to a new home. The builder was behind schedule—five months behind—and Gene and I were in a rental home living out of boxes. My computer was set up on the kitchen table and the fax machine was plugged into a wall behind the counter.

Then the deadline approached and the fax machine started churning out powerful life lessons about the influence of mothers from contributors all over the United States and beyond. Within a short time I knew this book had the potential of changing lives.

I salute the "construction crew":

### *The NavPress Publishing Team*
Thank you for giving me the freedom to try something new and for providing opportunities to brainstorm with your creative staff. I deeply appreciate your support and encouragement in ministry. Thanks, too, for the occasional gifts of flowers and chocolate. You make your authors feel valued!

Liz Heaney, if you weren't such a great editor, you'd make a superb architect! It's always painful when you revise and prune my manuscripts, but the end result is consistently better because of your input.

### *The Contributors*
Dynamic, gifted, overworked Christian leaders took time out of impossible schedules to write the stories in this book. The

result was more than I had hoped for. You made me laugh and cry, and I'll be a better mother because of you. Thank you for seeing the potential in this project and for being so honest and vulnerable.

### *The Local Team*

Gene Kent, you are my husband, best friend, and encourager. Thank you for listening to me read every story out loud and for moving our house and office twice while I finished this manuscript.

J.P., thanks for your uplifting calls and for bringing humor and hope to my life on a consistent basis. If your ears are ringing, it's because your mother is bragging about you again.

Laurie Dennis, you needed a "hard hat" to work for me during the past few months. Thank you for putting up with inadequate office space and for answering phone calls and doing all of the important behind-the-scenes jobs that allowed me to function in ministry during this year of transition. Your positive attitude gave me a daily "heart-lift!"

# Introduction

As the oldest of six children, I have rich memories of watching my mother deal with the daily emergencies and challenges of parenting. She was an early riser. I often peered down the big open staircase and saw her on her knees, praying out loud for each of us—by name. Mother taught important life lessons by example and always applied Scripture to everyday experiences.

As a speaker I have often used illustrations about my mother. One day an irate woman greeted me after a speech and gruffly said, "No wonder you could turn out so well. *You* had a godly heritage. Some of us just weren't that fortunate!" Abruptly, she turned on her heel and left.

I was hurt by the comment, but there was a truthful ring to the words. In our culture more than half of all marriages end in divorce. Many women are single parents. Some have come from nonChristian homes where they had no model of how to be a godly mother. And coming from a Christian home doesn't always mean there was good mothering. Even if we came from stable homes, most of us have days when we are miserable failures as moms!

Looking back, I realize most of the great ideas I learned about being a good mother came when other mothers (including my own) related specific incidents to me about raising their children or when they expressed how they dealt with daily emergencies. As I observed how they wove biblical teaching into the fabric of daily living, I became a better mother.

When the idea for this book became a reality, I asked Christian leaders all over the North American continent to contribute a story from their lives that demonstrates a life lesson their mothers taught them. It was sobering to have several decline because their mothers weren't positive examples in their lives. One well-known author and speaker said, "The only thing my mother and I had in common is that we both loved asparagus." When I pondered the tremendous achievements of this individual, I realized that *God can change the future generations, no matter what kind of a mother we've had, when we begin following biblical principles.* He can also give those of us from stable backgrounds creative, fresh ideas for being better mothers.

That's what this book is about. Expect to laugh out loud. And get your Kleenex box, too, because some of the stories are touching. Each vignette will demonstrate a life lesson based on a practical, common-sense, Bible-based principle. The title is *Mothers Have Angel Wings.* In the Bible angels were always messengers of God.

Try reading some of the stories to your children and then talk about the life lesson that is demonstrated in the illustration. Since a Scripture verse confirming the life lesson is printed at the end of each story, you can talk about how the illustration applies to your family.

Above all, prepare to *enjoy* yourself! This book is guaranteed to entertain you and inspire you at the same time! And if you'd like to write a tribute to your own mother, grandmother, or the woman who's been like a mom to you, you'll find a place to do that in the back of this book.

# Cross My Heart... and Hope to Die on the Spot!

LIZ CURTIS HIGGS

LIFE LESSON FROM MOTHER:
*Timing is everything.*

Sharon had one. Judy had one. Even Mary Ann had one, for crying out loud, and everybody could see *she* didn't need one yet.

Okay. I didn't need one either, but after that first gym class in seventh grade, it was clear the time had come.

I simply *had* to have a bra.

Some mothers made a big deal out of buying this particular foundational garment for their daughters. Judy's mom presented it to her in a pretty pink box filled with fluffy tissue paper and a special card: "Now that you're growing up . . ."

Mary Ann got a matching slip and panties with hers, in bright solid magenta. Mary Ann couldn't wear a white blouse for weeks.

Sharon and her mother went to the store to pick hers out. It was a special "trainer" model, AA, no batteries included, but it definitely counted. She was in.

And I was out. I was still underdeveloped enough for undershirts, but those went out of style with waist-high undies. Of course, I was still wearing those, too, but that wasn't the problem. The problem was the top half.

I casually mentioned buying a bra to Mother one day, who promptly "tsk-tsked" and assured me, "When you really need one, we'll buy you one." A quick check in the mirror told me the need level was low. *Flat* didn't even describe the situation. *Concave* was closer to the truth.

Secretly, I toyed with the idea of visiting Charlotte's Dress Shop on Main Street and buying one myself. *Oh, the adventure of it! I'd never been there alone . . . could I pull it off? Would Mom find out?*

One afternoon on the way home from school, after yet another humiliating "no show" in the locker room, I sneaked up the concrete steps and through the door into Charlotte's. The bell above the door tinkled loudly. I licked my dry lips, eyes darting about, as I prepared to ask a clerk the dreaded question: "Where are your . . . foundations?"

Thank goodness, there they were on full display. Not like the nylons Mother bought me, which came in little flat boxes stacked floor to ceiling behind the counter. No, these mysterious wonders were each in their own box with a see-through window. Just pick one out, march to the counter, plunk down your money . . . no problem!

Wait. Big problem . . . 32A? 34B? 36C? What in the world did *those* mean? I was an A-minus student; did I need an A-minus bra? As I peered at the confusing array, I sensed someone moving toward me and spun around to find Charlotte herself, a knowing smile on her lips, tape measure in hand.

"Were you looking for a particular size, dear?"

Gulp.

"Slip your coat off and let's see what we need, shall we?"

We needed a 32. Actually, we needed a 28, but they didn't make those. She measured at the full part, too. Twenty-eight inches. (For the record, my waist was also a 28.)

She chose the most promising box from the top corner

of the rack and pulled it out. A blush crept up my neck and around my ears as she directed me toward the dressing room. In a minute, she would know the truth: I didn't need a bra at all.

I think she noticed, but didn't say a word. "How does it feel?" she asked.

It felt like heaven. I smiled in the mirror, imagining my very own Playtex marvel making its debut at my next gym class. Never mind that the cups pooched out like empty pockets. I was finally going to be "in."

*"The most personal thing I ever said on the air had to do with my mother, who had recently died. I said that she wanted to go to college but there was no money, that she wanted to work but her husband wouldn't let her, and she wanted to go into politics but she knew no other women in politics. She said it wasn't her time. Instead, she pushed me to read (and) to stretch . . . She said it was my time."*

—LINDA ELLERBEE, TELEVISION JOURNALIST, *AND SO IT GOES*

"I think this will do, don't you?" Charlotte purred, heading for the register. "That'll be $7.95 plus tax. Shall I charge it on your mother's account?"

"No!" I almost shouted, then blinked back tears. *Seven dollars and ninety-five cents? I had no idea!* "No thanks,

I'll just . . . uh, come back for it tomorrow."

Undershirts were $2.50, tops. I had $4 to my name. Who could have imagined such an exorbitant price for something so . . . small? I dragged myself home, more discouraged than ever. No way was I bringing this up with Mom again. I would have to find another solution.

That solution was waiting for me in the trash can. My sister Mary, nine years my senior, had tossed out an old bra that had lost its zip. No question, it would take some effort to turn a 34B into a 28AAA, but I was desperate. Firing up our Singer sewing machine, I stitched the cups as flat as I could make them, added new seams to each side, and adjusted the shoulder straps.

*Ta-da!* It looked awful and felt worse, but if I moved fast in the locker room, no one would notice. I washed it by hand so Mother would never be the wiser and hid it in my closet to dry.

The next day in gym class, my pathetic excuse for a bra was nonetheless greeted with junior high enthusiasm—they even wrote a cheer to celebrate, along the lines of "Give me a B! Give me an R! Give me an A! . . ." I was delirious.

Got away with it, too, for nearly a week, until I carelessly tossed my makeshift bra in the laundry hamper Friday afternoon. By the time I remembered, Mom had gathered up the clothes and headed for the laundry room. I was toast for certain.

Mom never said a word. Not Saturday, not Sunday. I was in agony all weekend. Monday morning I found a plain white box on the top of the laundry basket. *Yikes! Mary's recycled bra with a stern note?*

I lifted the lid, grateful that no one was watching my hands as they shook. "Oh my!" I said aloud, my spirits lifting instantly. It was a brand new, lace-trimmed, ribbon-sporting brassiere, better than anything Charlotte's had to offer. Perfect for a young lady in training.

A voice from the doorway brought up my head with a snap. "I realized it was time," Mom said, smiling slightly, watching me with something like regret in her eyes. "Welcome to womanhood, honey."

I didn't trust myself to speak, so instead I pressed my cheek against hers and squeezed my eyes tightly enough to hold back the tears. Finally I managed to whisper, "Thanks, Mom."

My mother almost never laughed out loud, but that day she did. "Don't thank me for *that,* daughter dear! You'll be anxious to get rid of them soon enough, believe me."

As usual, Mom was right.

*There is a time for everything,*
*and a season for every activity under heaven.*
Ecclesiastes 3:1

# Do What?

CAROLE MAYHALL

LIFE LESSON FROM MOTHER:
*Responding to anger with kindness works!*

Joyce was a small explosive brunette with a temper the size of an atomic cloud, and just about as dangerous. She was certainly not one to cross! I'd seen her fly at a school chum, fingers clawing the air as though she had every intention of digging out the girl's eyes.

In the course of events, our seventh-grade teacher left the room for a few minutes and put me in charge as the monitor. (Horrible thing to do!) Joyce immediately began acting up. I asked her as nicely as I could to please stop disrupting the class. She didn't. And so I was forced to report her conduct to the teacher who in turn gave Joyce a stern lecture in front of the class.

If looks were daggers, Joyce would have cut me to ribbons. As she brushed by my desk, she hissed, "Just you wait until recess this afternoon!" In my imagination, I saw a banshee-from-hell ripping my dress and pulling out my hair.

At noon I fled home for lunch, scared and miserable.

Mom sensed that something was wrong and asked, "Honey, what's the matter? What happened?"

I poured out my tale of woe.

Mom listened calmly, thought a moment, and then said, "Carole, take her an apple."

"Take her an apple?" I wailed. "What good will *that* do? She's ready to pull out my hair! And besides, *I* didn't do anything wrong. *She* did!"

"I know, Carole. But the Bible says to 'do good to those who are spiteful to you.' It also says that a 'soft answer turns away wrath.' I don't think it can hurt, and perhaps it will help. Try it!" Then she reached into the refrigerator, pulled out a big red apple, shined it until it gleamed, and handed it to me.

*"Kind words can be short and easy to speak but their echoes are truly endless."*

—MOTHER TERESA, QUOTED IN *RANDOM ACTS OF KINDNESS*

"Why don't you walk into school, put this apple on Joyce's desk, and just say, 'I'm sorry you are so angry,' and see what happens."

I wrestled with her suggestion, but in the end I marched into class after lunch, stepped up to Joyce's desk and put the apple before her, and mumbled, "I'm sorry you are so angry."

Joyce's eyes widened and her mouth dropped open. Wordless for a moment, she finally stammered, "Well . . . well . . . er . . ." and then finished lamely, "I guess I deserved it."

Situation diffused, Joyce and I eventually grew to be friends.

The concept of doing something nice for someone who doesn't like you or has something against you stayed with me as I saw Mom live out that concept. When a jealous lady at church began spreading ugly and untrue rumors about

Mom, Mother sent her a red rose every day for a week with an encouraging Scripture verse on the card. It wasn't long before that woman became one of Mom's most staunch defenders.

Our natural inclination when someone is angry or hateful is to retreat or fight back. But Mom taught the supernatural command of Jesus, "But I tell you . . . do good to those who hate you, bless those who curse you, pray for those who mistreat you" (Luke 6:27-28).

Don't tell anyone, but I have a feeling that Mom, now in heaven, is praying that I'll practice that command more and more frequently *even now!*

> *"Here is a simple rule of thumb for behavior:*
> *Ask yourself what you want people to do for you;*
> *then grab the initiative and do it for them!*
> *If you only love the lovable, do you expect*
> *a pat on the back? Run-of-the-mill sinners do that. . . .*
> *I tell you, love your enemies. Help and give*
> *without expecting a return. You'll never—I promise—*
> *regret it. Live out this God-created identity*
> *the way our Father lives toward us,*
> *generously and graciously, even when*
> *we're at our worst. Our Father is kind;*
> *you be kind."*
> Luke 6:31-36, MSG

# The Treasured Letter

CAROL KENT

LIFE LESSON FROM MOTHER:
*Affirm your love with tangible evidence.*

It's dog-eared, yellowed, and stained with water marks—perhaps the tears of the letter writer or the receiver. The stationery is ordinary. No fancy logo or embossed return address. Just a simple note I will cherish always. It's the letter my mother wrote to me the day before my wedding. She presented it to me with love and joy.

Enveloped in the warmth of her embrace, this is what I read:

*Dear Carol,*

*I feel very close to you tonight. I just want to write my thoughts about you down on paper. I'm remembering how I longed for a child of my own. Even before I was married, I dreamed of the day when I'd have a little girl of my own. I'll never forget the day I found out I was going to have you. I was very close to the Lord at that time. I talked to Him often about the child He would commit to my keeping. Before you were ever born you were dedicated to my Lord Jesus Christ.*

*When you arrived, they told me I had a baby girl with red fuzzy hair, weighing 5 lb. 14 oz., 21 inches long. I was too thrilled for words! My first thought was, "Is she normal?" My second thought was, "Thank you, Lord, for my own little baby girl." I could hardly believe* it could be possible. Me with a little baby girl. How good God was to me!

I whispered to you and talked to you and told you again and again about Jesus right from the start. As you grew older you'd smile as though you really understood what I was saying.

Time passed and then came your first day of school, piano lessons for which you hated to practice, and finally that day on the farm when we sat listening to the radio program, "Unshackled." When it was over you were crying and told me you were such a sinner. There on our knees that tremendous transaction was made and you were born again into God's family.

You were growing up so fast and we had many precious times of prayer together. Then came your first date, and eventually Gene entered your life as a boyfriend. His interest in spiritual things and his hunger for the Word of God made me love him very soon. Then you were off to college and the next four years of your life seemed to fly by.

I was so happy when you became engaged to Gene. I think I loved him long before you did. Now the time for your marriage has arrived. This is your last night in our home as my little Carol Joy Afman. Soon you'll be a married woman. I face this night with mixed emotions. I'm so happy for you both, but there will be an empty place here. Always remember how much I love you.

May God's richest blessings be yours. Always put Him first. Pray much about your relationship to one another before God. Don't neglect the family altar, and you just have to be the happiest married couple this side of heaven.

Love and Prayers,

Mother

With that letter my mother affirmed her love for me, reminded me of my early commitment to Christ, valued my choice of a husband, and gave me wise counsel upon which to build a marriage. That treasured letter still warms my heart and makes my eyes brim with tears. *I know I am loved.*

*"I sat down on the couch and ran my fingers around the string of forty-eight faux pearls (my mother's pearls). And as I did, those small, smooth gems became, for me, touchstones—linking me to the memories of a godly woman who lived her simple life in a way that witnessed God's glory."*

—Daisy Hepburn, *Forget Not His Blessings*

*"I have loved you with an everlasting love; I have drawn you with loving-kindness."*
Jeremiah 31:3

# The Pixie Dust Extravaganza

DOTTIE MCDOWELL

LIFE LESSON FROM MOTHER:
*Dreaming our children's dreams
communicates in a powerful way how
much we delight in them.*

When I was a little girl, Peter Pan was my hero. Each time I heard about the boy who could fly, I felt inspired and energized. The story took my breath away, and I spent much time living and reliving each scene. I couldn't get enough of it.

*"Dreams are the touchstones
of our characters."*

—HENRY THOREAU, *GREAT QUOTES & ILLUSTRATIONS*

I remember the day I wandered down into our basement when I was about five years old. Near my mother's washing machine, I spotted a large box of Ivory Snow. In my well-developed imagination, each beautiful flake looked like the pixie dust Tinkerbell used to sprinkle on Wendy, Michael, and John to enable them to fly.

Overcome with excitement, I knew that I could relive Tinkerbell's scene. I'll never forget the exhilaration I felt as I took handfuls of pixie dust and sprinkled them generously throughout the entire basement. It was magical. When I was done, *everything* was covered with soap. When my mom discovered what I had done, she lovingly listened to my childish fantasy and dreams and recognized how much the experience meant to me. Instead of getting angry or frustrated, she laughed with me and encouraged me to repeat the whole story of Peter Pan to her. Later, lightheartedly, we cleaned up the enormous mess together.

From that day to this, the memory of my "pixie dust extravaganza" reminds me that my mom dreamed my dreams. I was important to her. She unselfishly chose to support and encourage my dreams—even childish ones—over her own interests or convenience.[1]

*He has led me to a place of safety;*
*He rescued me because He delights in me.*

Psalm 18:19, NLT

# Moving Forward

SANDRA PICKLESIMER ALDRICH

LIFE LESSON FROM MOTHER:
*Allowing God to lead your children spares
hurt feelings and results in lasting
accomplishments.*

Whenever I want to give my young adult children advice about how they *should* handle a particular situation, I try to take a deep breath and pray, as I remember the example my mother, Wilma Picklesimer, set several years ago.

My thirty-nine-year-old husband, Don, had died just a few days after Christmas in 1982. It took fifteen months before I was ready to take down the single bed that had been mine since the cancer diagnosis and return to the double bed Don and I had shared all the years before his illness. After his death, I found it less traumatic to just ignore the big bed—and the resulting clutter—and to continue sleeping in my single bed.

Suddenly, one overcast morning, I decided it was time to turn the bedroom from "ours" into "mine," and with my eleven-year-old son helping, I tackled the chore with determination. About an hour into the job, the phone rang. It was my mother.

"You sound out of breath," she said. "Did you have to run up the stairs to answer?"

"No. Jay and I were just shoving furniture around. I've taken down the single bed and was rearranging my bedroom."

I could hear her crying softly.

"What's wrong?" I asked.

No answer. Just more sniffs.

"Mother, please don't. You know I can't stand it when you cry long distance. I'm only rearranging furniture."

Finally she said, "It's just that the Lord answered my prayer. When I was over there two weeks ago and helped you fold the laundry, I looked at that crowded room and asked the Lord to help you move on. And every morning for two weeks I've asked Him to nudge you to rearrange that room."

*"The mother eagle teaches her little ones to fly by making their nest so uncomfortable they are forced to leave it and commit themselves to the unknown world of the air outside. And just so does our God to us. He stirs up our comfortable nests, and pushes us over the edge of them, and we are forced to use our wings to save ourselves from fatal falling . . . Your wings are being developed."*

—HANNAH WHITALL SMITH,
*THE CHRISTIAN'S SECRET OF A HAPPY LIFE*

That startled me, of course, but it also got me to thinking. What if she had marched into my home and announced, "Okay, you've ignored this room long enough. It's time to get on with your life." Obviously, it wouldn't have worked, since the "letting go" would have been from her direction rather than my own readiness.

Instead, she just prayed, trusting the Lord to move me forward. And that's what I try to hold onto as I watch my own grown children struggle at times. Allowing Him to lead them not only spares hurt feelings but results in lasting accomplishments.

*Don't exasperate your children*
*by coming down hard on them.*
*Take them by the hand and lead them*
*in the way of the Master.*
Ephesians 6:4, MSG

# The Gift-Giver

SANDY PETRO

LIFE LESSON FROM MOTHER:
*It is more fulfilling to give than to receive.*

As I emptied a closet next to my daughter's room, I found
her Raggedy Ann. Not an ordinary Raggedy Ann, but a
handmade doll, lovingly made, and filled with Grandma's
handiwork.

"Shannon," I called, "can you come here a minute?"
My sixteen-year-old daughter came around the corner. "Sit
down," I said. "Let me tell you once again how special this
doll is."

My daughter and I began to reminisce about MaMaw
and how she enjoyed spoiling her only granddaughter
with gifts she could lovingly make by hand. This Raggedy
Ann was the last gift MaMaw made before she died. We
recalled how the doll was not quite complete when
MaMaw was taken to the hospital. When she realized she
might not be able to do the finishing touches herself, she
paid someone to finish it to her liking.

It was Shannon's second birthday, and MaMaw's face
lit up as she awarded that doll to her precious granddaughter. We all laughed as Shannon squealed with delight
to hug a new friend who was as tall as she was! MaMaw
died soon after that birthday celebration, but not before
she etched in our hearts and minds the true meaning of
the gift of giving.

The phone rang, jolting us into the present. Shannon
left to answer the call, and I slipped back into memories

of MaMaw that she had woven for me with the threads of her talent, love, and giving heart.

I remembered my best friend, Carol, and me at eight years old, twirling around in matching dresses that revealed full lace petticoats underneath. Mother had made them. She often made something for Carol to match what she stitched for me. "I had a little extra material," she would say.

*"I remember the night*
*that I came to you late . . .*
*and told you that I was supposed to be*
*a king in a play at school the next day.*
*Somehow you rose to the occasion*
*and created a king's purple robe . . .*
*I knew then that you were a mother*
*like no other . . . but I didn't realize*
*what a great lady you were."*

—TIM HANSEL, QUOTED BY ALICE GRAY IN *STORIES FOR THE HEART*

I smelled the aromas of pies, cakes, casseroles, and other goodies that my mother carried to the neighbors. "Welcome to the neighborhood," she would say. Or, "I know you've been working a lot of hours lately. I thought you might enjoy this." My mother worked outside the home, too, but she always found time to give to others.

I felt the soft stems of deep purple violets in my hands as I remembered how every year, when I was in grade school, my mother would take me to a nearby riverbank to pick violets for my teacher. I laughed to myself, remembering how she did most of the picking herself. It was a tedious job to make a large bouquet out of violets. "Hold the vase tightly," she would say, as she put me on the school bus.

I heard the click of my mother's favorite sewing scissors as she painstakingly cut miniature shapes out of leftover fabrics she had used to make clothes for me. These small pieces of material were transformed into spectacular, detailed wardrobes for dolls that were auctioned off every year at my grade school fundraising events.

Every year I heard "oohs" and "ahhs" as the girls gathered around to inspect the newly completed collection. What did they admire most? The double-breasted blue-plaid wool coat with the matching hat and gold buttons? The soft, pink flannel pajamas with lace trim and appliquéd satin hearts? The red party dress with the layers of ruffles and big puffed sleeves? The multicolored underwear embroidered with the days of the week? Each year's wardrobe seemed more remarkable than the last.

The organizational committee for the fall festival always wanted to recognize my mother before these auctions began, but she always said no. Mother repeatedly minimized her months of work and was content for her gift to be anonymous.

Shannon stuck her head in the door, interrupting my memories. "Mom, that was Linda on the phone. She's coming to help you clean on Thursday. I cleaned out my closet yesterday and put all the things I've outgrown in a bag. Could we give them to Linda for her daughter?"

I nodded yes. As Shannon left I smiled to myself, and with a final glance at Raggedy Ann, I said, "Mom, your gift of giving has become a legacy that lives on!"

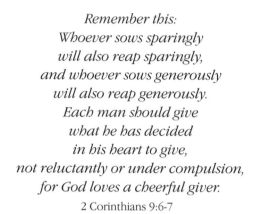

*Remember this:*
*Whoever sows sparingly*
*will also reap sparingly,*
*and whoever sows generously*
*will also reap generously.*
*Each man should give*
*what he has decided*
*in his heart to give,*
*not reluctantly or under compulsion,*
*for God loves a cheerful giver.*
2 Corinthians 9:6-7

# Mrs. McGillicutty's Band-Aids

LUAN ZEMMER JACKSON, MS, RN

LIFE LESSON FROM GRANDMA:
*Nurture the potential in every child.*

When I was two-and-a-half years old my father was the pastor of a small country church. On weekdays he was a medical student in the city, and on weekends he returned home to tend to his church duties. We lived in a small country house without running water or indoor plumbing. God met our need for food and clothing through the gifts of generous people.

Life was hard. My grandma (the bright spot in my life) lived across the road. Every day I would dress up in my best outfit and knock on her door. Grandma greeted me as if I were the most important company she ever entertained. She had a magnificent imagination and created imaginary scenarios that took me far beyond my current circumstances.

Our favorite game transformed us into neighbors. Grandma was Mrs. McGillicutty and I was Mrs. Zemmer. In European style we had tea and talked about our children. (Grandma had six children and I had my dolls.) I always felt important and grown up when I visited Grandma. She asked for my advice on dealing with her problems and listened intently to my answers. I knew Grandma loved me and valued my advice.

Rainy days made me a prisoner at home and kept Grandma's world out of reach. On one occasion, after several days of rain, I persuaded my mother to let me go to Grandma's. As I crossed the road, I fell into a massive mud puddle. Sitting in that cold, murky water, covered with slimy mud, I started to cry. Embarrassment and shame overwhelmed me. How could I have been so careless? My good dress was filthy. My knee was scraped and hurting. What would Grandma say?

From her yard on the other side of the road, Grandma saw my plight, came across the road, and rescued me. With a smile she said, "Don't cry, Luan, we'll get you all cleaned up. Your dress will be fine and we'll put a Band-Aid on that knee."

Grandma talked to me as she cleaned my wounds. "Luan, I want you to remember how embarrassed you feel—and how your knee hurts. Other people hurt sometimes, too. It feels good to have someone take care of you, doesn't it? Remember that others have hurts and need to be cared for."

After that incident I became a "ministering angel." I started a doll hospital. My friends played house with their dolls, but I had a new mission—to help people who needed my services. I waited for someone to get hurt—a neighbor, family member, or stranger—and rushed in to cleanse the wound and apply a Band-Aid.

In those days of economic hardship, money was precious, but Grandma kept me well supplied with Band-Aids. Well-meaning adults told Grandma she was wasting valuable resources to buy Band-Aids for a child to play with, but she continued to supply me with resources for my little nurse's bag. Because of Grandma, whenever someone had a wound, I would confidently care for them.

Grandma's words still ring in my ears, "You are so caring, Luan. It's comforting to have you here to take care of us!" Mrs. McGillicutty and Mrs. Zemmer continued to have tea together for many years. Grandma helped me envision an exciting and fulfilling future. "When you grow up," she said, "you will be a great nurse, because nurses are caring just like you and they take care of hurting people just like you do." In between sips of tea, she complimented me on my communication skills and encouraged my sense of humor. "In a world full of pain, we need to laugh and help others to laugh," she would say with a chuckle.

*"Everybody should try to have
a grandmother, especially if they don't have
a television, because they are the only
grown-ups who have time."*

—Excerpt from an essay by a third grade student from Langley, BC

Somewhere between having tea and distributing Band-Aids, I determined that with God's help (and Grandma's encouragement), I would get an education. Grandma was honest about her poor choices. "When I was young, I listened to my friends talking about marriage. I wanted to be a nurse, but I hid my dream and did what everyone else was doing. Marriage is wonderful, but you need an education first. In order to be a good nurse, you will need to attend college." She added, "Never give up!"

Grandma saw beyond the little girl in the mud puddle

and believed in my potential. She gave wings to my dreams by supplying me with Band-Aids. And she passed on a legacy of love that is being transferred to the next generation through my children today.

By the way, Mrs. Zemmer *did* become a nurse and today she owns and operates a full-service mental health clinic. And she misses having tea with Mrs. McGillicutty.

*The people brought children to Jesus,*
*hoping he might touch them.*
*The disciples shooed them off. But Jesus was irate*
*and let them know it: "Don't push these children away.*
*Don't ever get between them and me.*
*These children are at the very center of life*
*in the kingdom. Mark this:*
*Unless you accept God's kingdom in the simplicity*
*of a child, you'll never get in."*
*Then, gathering the children up in his arms,*
*he laid his hands of blessing on them.*
Mark 10:13-16, MSG

# Do It Right!

CYNTHIA HEALD

LIFE LESSON FROM MOTHER:
*If you are going to do
anything, do it right.*

How often I heard my mother say, "Cynthia Ann, if you are going to do something, take the time to do it right."

I learned early on

- to set the table correctly
- to iron so that my dress looked nice
- to respond to people with respect
- to study well.

My mother was not a perfectionist, and she never made me feel that what I did was inferior. At the heart of her teaching was the principle that if I chose to do anything, then I should do my best. She taught me that doing something right the first time *saved* time, because I never had to go back and do it over again.

Probably the first time this lesson took was when I learned to wash dishes. If Mom found a dish that had not been properly washed (this was "BD"—*before dishwashers!*), she would lovingly and patiently show me how to check the dishes for cleanliness. Then she would say, "Now, honey, if you are going to do something, take your time and do it right."

Her advice influenced me as a student. When I did my homework or wrote a paper, I always thought, "If I'm going to spend time studying, then I want to do it right— otherwise, why study?"

Her words had an impact on me as a wife. I thought, "If I'm going to be married, then I want to be the best wife I can be. I want to do it right."

Her wisdom shaped my choices as a mother. Again, I thought, "If I'm going to spend all this time raising children, then I want to be the best mother I can be."

But most of all, I took her teaching to heart in my relationship with God. I am still "in process" and far from perfect, but my thoughts concerning my walk with God have always been along this line: "Lord, since I am yours, I want to be all that you want me to be. I don't want to play around or waste time. I want to be wholehearted and I want to do what is right as your child."

*"Some people have greatness
thrust upon them. Very few have excellence
thrust upon them . . . They achieve it.
They do not achieve it unwittingly
by doing what comes naturally,
and they don't stumble into it
in the course of amusing themselves.
All excellence involves discipline
and the tenacity of purpose."*

—JOHN W. GARDNER, *GREAT QUOTES & ILLUSTRATIONS*

All of this seemed to culminate as I was turning forty years old. I suddenly realized the shortness of life and that in all probability, my life was half over. As I was reading through the book of Ruth that year, I was amazed by Boaz's comment to Ruth, "And now, my daughter, do not fear. I will do for you whatever you ask, for all my people in the city know that you are a woman of excellence" (Ruth 3:11, NASB). I thought, *Here is a woman of virtue, of strength, of excellence. She was a widow gleaning day after day in barley fields for her mother-in-law. Even though her life was difficult and far from spectacular, Ruth was committed to doing whatever she did in an excellent way.*

Because of what my mother taught me and because of God's Spirit within me, I'm committed to spending the rest of my life being in the process of becoming *a woman of excellence.*

Thanks, Mom, for doing it right!

*Whether, then, you eat or drink*
*or whatever you do,*
*do all to the glory of God.*
1 Corinthians 10:31, NASB

# The First Place Ribbon

CYNTHIA SPELL HUMBERT

LIFE LESSON FROM MOTHER:
*Self-worth should not be based
on the opinions of others,
but on God's view of who we are.*

When I was eleven, I was convinced I stood a foot taller than all the boys in my class and wondered if I'd always weigh eighty-nine pounds. And I worried about *when* and *if* my teeth would ever look right in my face. I knew I would never be voted "Most Popular" or "Miss Personality" in my sixth-grade class, but I was yet to learn how much pain children could inflict on each other.

I learned all too well one Friday afternoon. I had just been awarded the First Place Ribbon for the Elementary Music Contest. I felt proud. My hard work and practice had paid off. But as my classmates lined up to leave the auditorium, someone in the crowd started chanting: "We want Tina! We want Tina!"

Tina, the class favorite, hadn't won, but my peers made it clear that she was their choice for the winner—not me!

My mother was there that day, and she was waiting for me at home with open arms after school. She shared my pain and let me cry about the brokenness of my heart.

Mother took me for a walk in the woods surrounding our home. We talked about the medley I had sung from the *Sound of Music* that had won the contest that day. She reminded me of a song Julie Andrews sings in the movie when she's feeling overwhelmed and frightened called, "I Have Confidence."

So, hand-in-hand my mother and I walked through those woods, belting out the words to the melody I had sung earlier. It was a song about going after the things you're dreaming of and having courage in the middle of life's struggles. As we sang the lyrics at the top of our lungs, I believed the words and was powerfully encouraged by the theme. Instead of feeling insecure and unpopular, I felt *confident*!

*"When we have experienced*
*the power of mother love,*
*we not only have higher self-esteem*
*and a greater capacity for trust*
*and intimacy than those who have not,*
*but we also have a different life experience*
*than those who were, and continue to be,*
*maternally deprived."*

—Dr. Brenda Hunter,
In the Company of Women

After finishing the song, we talked through the truth about confidence. It wasn't some fuzzy feeling that when the going got tough, the tough sang a little ditty and felt better. True confidence came from knowing that no matter how other people treated me, God dearly loved me, and my worth as a person was based in Him.

It wasn't easy to return to school. I can't count the

times when life has seemed overwhelming and I've held my chin up and internally belted out that song. But what my mother imprinted on my mind is still recorded there—that I can be confident because God is our ever-present help in times of trouble.

*There has never been the slightest doubt in my mind that the God who started this great work in you would keep at it and bring it to a flourishing finish on the very day Christ Jesus appears.*
Philippians 1:6, MSG

# I Forgave You So Long Ago

JENNIE AFMAN DIMKOFF

LIFE LESSON FROM MOTHER:
*Forgive sooner rather than later,
remembering all the Savior
has forgiven you.*

I was homesick. Deeply, painfully, and overwhelmingly homesick.

My husband was in the army and we were sent far from our home state of Michigan to Ft. Polk, Louisiana.

I desperately missed my mother. I remembered her tenderness and the times she had sacrificed for me. I thought of the countless mornings I had come down the stairs and found her on her knees at our old, worn-out couch, praying out loud for her children. I didn't just *miss* her, I was haunted by the memory of how many times I made her cry when I was a teenager.

I was a good student and very involved in my high school. Life was exciting, and I was a platform person. I loved the spotlight. But our house had no stage or spotlight. I lived in a parsonage with a family of eight on a limited budget. I resented the workload that came with being one of the oldest, and I was unhappy with the scarcity of money. I objected to the strict rules and curfew my parents required. I verbally abused my mom.

"Why are you so unfair? I have the lead in the school musical and you make me come home from the play party by midnight! Are you trying to humiliate me in front of my friends, or is it that you don't trust me?"

"Why do I have to vacuum the whole downstairs before I leave for school every morning? And when I get home from school there's a sink full of dirty dishes to wash before we even have supper! What do you do all day, anyway?!"

I had many grievances, and when the front door was closed—and especially if my dad wasn't there—I had a harsh and selfish tongue that I exercised on my mother. For some reason, she let me get away with saying those hateful things, but sometimes she cried.

*"God pardons like a mother who kisses away the repentant tears of her child."*

—HENRY WARD BEECHER, QUOTED IN *A RAINBOW OF HOPE*

Years later, there I was—a grown woman, established in my own home, far away, missing her, and miserable that I had made her grieve.

Four years passed. My husband was nearing the completion of his military service and we needed to find a home and office space for his legal practice. We decided to go home to Michigan for a quick trip during my Easter break from teaching. I wrote ahead to Mother, inviting her to come down from the Upper Peninsula to meet us. She drove the six-hour trip all by herself so that we could be together, and it was a wonderful visit.

Later in the week, after a meeting with our realtor, I left my husband downtown and drove back to the home where we were staying. No other vehicles were in the driveway and I figured I had the place to myself. I went in the back door, through the kitchen, and stopped. There sat Mother in a rocking chair in the living room. Her head was back and her eyes were closed. She was sound asleep. I stood there in the doorway and watched her for a while.

*I love her so much,* I thought. *Oh, how I've missed her.* I realized the time had come for me to make something right that had been very wrong for a long time.

I knelt beside her chair and gently laid my elbow in her lap. As she woke up, I rested my head against my arm. She tenderly stroked my hair as though I were a little girl again.

"Oh, Mom, I've missed you so much!"

"I've missed you too, honey," she said, caressing my cheek.

I straightened to look up into her eyes. "Mom, there's something that's been bothering me for a long time and I have to ask you to forgive me."

"Forgive you? Whatever for?"

"Oh Mom, for all those times I made you cry when I was a teenager. I didn't understand that when you were strict you were trying to protect me. I was so full of myself. I didn't have any real understanding of Dad's ministry or that it was our *family* ministry, too. You had a houseful of children, and it was *my* part of the ministry to vacuum every morning. When dirty dishes were waiting in the sink after school, it was because you'd been dishing out prayer, counseling, and apple pie to spiritually-needy people all afternoon. I was so selfish. I hurt you so many times. Please forgive me, Mama. I am so sorry."

Through tears of her own, my mother embraced me and quietly replied, "Oh, my dear Jennie—I love you, and I forgave you so long ago, so very long ago."

Many years have passed since that refreshing day, but I have been grateful countless times since for the lesson Mother taught me by modeling God's forgiveness. When I go to my heavenly Father with a broken and contrite heart and say, "Oh God, I'm so sorry. I blew it. I have hurt you *again.* Please forgive me," the Savior looks at me through all the love that prompted him to go to Calvary and He says, "Oh my child, I love you. I have loved you since before you were born, and I paid the price for that so long ago. You're forgiven."

*Forgive as quickly and completely*
*as the Master forgave you.*
Colossians 3:13b, MSG

# An Ugly, Old, Beautiful Woman

BECKY FREEMAN

LIFE LESSON FROM MOTHER:
*Part of a woman's beauty comes from the ability to enjoy a good laugh at one's self.*

Everyone who sees my mother, Ruthie, remarks on her beauty. She is petite, with a waist size Scarlett O'Hara would have envied. With her high cheekbones and stylish silver hair, she grows more striking as the years pass. My husband, Scott, often winks when he sees his mother-in-law, teasing that he decided to marry me when he saw my mother. It's precisely my mother's physical attractiveness that makes the following "Ruthie Story" such fun to repeat.

---

We were vacationing at Holly Lake, our favorite family vacation spot in the piney woods of east Texas. One morning Mother decided to enjoy her coffee on the porch of our rented mobile home. We kids disappeared into the woods to do our own thing, and she propped up her feet, soaking in the peace and quiet. Before long, a small dog that looked more like a rag mop than a dog frolicked down the path and up onto the porch, giving Mother his "jumpin', lickin' dawg" greeting. Scarcely had she wiped the slobber off her feet when the dog's mistress came into view, breathless with apology as she attempted to corner her "naughty boy."

Mother guessed the woman to be about her age, but while Mother was clad in her robe and no makeup, this lady was clad (just barely) in a lime-green bikini and fur-lined boots. The extent of her tan indicated the bikini was her most frequent costume, which indicated to Mother that they might not have a lot in common. Even so, they struck up a conversation in which Mother became the primary listener.

The topic centered on the lady's daughter, of whom she was extremely proud because she worked as a hostess in a famous nightclub (now defunct) in Dallas where she was required to wear a small costume resembling a rabbit. Mother's new acquaintance expected to marry again soon, and her fiancé had a motto: "You can tell a successful man by how expensive his toys are." Furthermore, she owned her own business in Dallas, and she knew the score.

"I don't hire young, cute women," she declared. "They're nothing but trouble in an office. They fuss with each other and the men can't keep their minds on their work. I hire ugly, old women." She then shrewdly looked Mother over, sized her up, and paid her the supreme compliment. "I'd hire *you*."

*"You don't stop laughing because you grow old, you grow old because you stop laughing.*

—A Bumper Sticker, quoted by Barbara Johnson in *Stick a Geranium in Your Hat and Be Happy!*

As you can imagine we kids loved teasing our pretty mother about being an "ugly old woman." But no one enjoyed telling the story more than Mother herself—and always, she'd end up laughing the most.[1]

*A cheerful heart brings a smile to your face.*

Proverbs 15:13, MSG

*A cheerful disposition is good for your health;*
*gloom and doom leave you bone-tired.*

Proverbs 17:22, MSG

# The Day
# I Wanted to Quit

Carol Kent

LIFE LESSON FROM MOTHER:
*Prayer is the most powerful tool we have.*

The woman on the phone sounded very professional. "Carol, we've just found your name, speaking topics, and qualifications in a listing from the National Speakers Association. We are calling to find out if you're free to speak for our women's conference." The caller said I'd be needed for four days in a row during a summer conference held at a beautiful resort overlooking the sandy shores of Lake Michigan.

"We'd like for you to give four talks on the topic of *The Spiritual Dimension of Your Life*," she said.

I could hardly believe my ears! I always tried to keep a few dates open in my calendar to speak for business and professional groups. Although most of my speaking was in Christian circles, this outlet enabled me to be "salt" in the real world. I was more than surprised to be asked to speak about something spiritual at a secular women's conference.

Before the woman hung up, she said, "If your husband can get some vacation time, bring your family along. They will enjoy the resort while you're working—and you'll have lots of free time together."

We made the proper arrangements, and with happy hearts we embarked on our journey to the conference center. It was everything she promised. Beautiful accommodations. Sandy beaches. Perfect weather. A true paradise.

The first day of my participation, I arrived just before one of the other speakers addressed the group and slipped into a seat on the back row. As she began her presentation, I looked around, trying to get a feel for what kind of group I would be speaking to later. I was jarred to alertness as I heard the speaker announce vigorously: "I believe a family is a group of sick people who live together, with the sickest member of the group in control."

Women in the audience were applauding and bellowing, "Yea! Bravo!"

The speaker continued with enthusiasm. "I believe the only reason a woman ever gets married is because she has low self-esteem and can't make decisions. Some man comes riding along on his white horse, swoops her out of her circumstances, and she never gets to make another decision for herself as long as she lives."

The more I heard the more concerned I became. What had I gotten myself into? At the end of her talk they gave her a standing ovation. Until that moment, I had no idea I had accepted an invitation to speak to a group of militant feminists!

After a short break, I was introduced as the next speaker. I mounted the platform and began with one of my favorite humorous introductions. The women were laughing and the atmosphere was warm. But as soon as I started to address the topic of spirituality, the audience response changed dramatically. I spoke with conviction, describing my own spiritual journey and explaining how personal faith in Jesus Christ had provided a foundation for happiness and fulfillment in life. As I glanced up from my notes, most of the women had crossed their arms in defiance.

I could feel their hostility. For the first time in my adult Christian life I experienced what the Bible means when it says, "The man without the Spirit does not accept the things that come from the Spirit of God, for they are foolishness to him, and he cannot understand them, because they are spiritually discerned" (1 Corinthians 2:14).

When I finished there was no applause; no participants were shrieking, "Bravo!" As women stood up and filed out of the room, I heard the muffled rumble of antagonistic remarks. Suddenly, the woman who had spoken earlier came up to me, rose to a rigid posture, glared with steely gray eyes, and said, "Well, that's not exactly what we were expecting to hear!"

I chose my words carefully. "The meeting planner asked me to speak on *The Spiritual Dimension of Your Life,* and that's the topic I've tried to address."

With an arrogant sneer, she taunted, "If you ask me, you're a little more *spiritual* than what we wanted." She pivoted and marched out of the room.

My heart raced. A nervous flush began creeping up my neck. My breathing was labored, and I choked back a sob as tears threatened to reveal my total humiliation and insecurity.

When the room had emptied, I raced back to my room and curled up in the embryo position, weeping like a baby in front of my baffled husband and son, J. P. I wailed to them, "I'm never going to speak publicly again for the rest of my life. It's too hard. They're too mean. I feel like an idiot and a failure. They were looking for a new age presentation on spirituality, and I told them about Jesus, and they hate me. I can't face them again! *And I will not subject myself to this level of embarrassment and humiliation again!*"

When I finished, Gene quietly placed his hand on my shoulder and said, "But Carol, you've signed a contract."

I had signed a legally binding agreement to speak to this group for *three more days!* I ached with misery.

A couple of hours later Gene gently woke me from a fitful sleep. It was time for dinner—and all of our meals were scheduled in a central dining room with the conference participants. I was convinced I couldn't eat a thing, and I certainly didn't have the courage to face those women. Gene insisted that it would be much easier to build bridges over a meal than to disappear until I had to do the next presentation.

*"Prayer does not equip us for greater works—prayer is the greater work."*

—OSWALD CHAMBERS, QUOTED IN *A RAINBOW OF HOPE*

As we walked up the main sidewalk, Gene held open the door of the dining room for J. P. and me. Some of the conferees were also approaching the entrance. J. P. and I looked back to see a humorous sight. With mischievous, sparkling eyes, Gene flashed them his radiant, full-teeth grin and spoke with his most dynamic *insurance salesman* voice, "Good evening, ladies!"

One of the women grabbed the doorknob out of his hand and said, "Thank you, but we do that for *ourselves* around here!"

A couple of hours later, I called my dear mother. I needed her comfort . . . and her prayer. Mom keeps a list of my speaking engagements and bathes those ministry opportunities with prayer. As she picked up the receiver on the other end of the line, I whimpered, "Mom? Is that you?"

"Carol, what is going on with you at that conference? The oddest thing is happening here. I've been working around the house, sometimes in the kitchen, sometimes in one of the bedrooms, when suddenly and very directly God puts the burden on my heart that you need prayer. I've had to drop everything I'm doing and go to my knees on your behalf until I've sensed that you were all right. I've rarely felt so compelled to pray fervently for a specific need. *What is happening?*"

I began to cry. Never before had I experienced what it's like to have God lay the burden of *my* need on someone else's heart. I felt overwhelming thankfulness for prayer and a deep reverence for my powerful God who understood my pain and my impossible task.

After recounting the details to Mom, I told her about the contract I'd signed. She measured her words carefully and then responded. "Honey, you can do it. Be like Daniel in the lions' den. *You go and speak to those women and I'll pray.*" Mother finished the call by praying aloud for me.

As I hung up I knew that I would be okay. With God's help I could do this. My courage had returned. I would not be alone on that platform. The One I had to please was my Maker, not my audience. And my dear mama would be praying.

Each time I mounted the stage for the next three days my heart pounded, but I boldly spoke of true spirituality.

By the end of the conference, many of the women were warming up to my family and appeared genuinely interested in the messages. When I voiced disappointment to Mother that I'd seen no decisions for Christ, she reminded me that "planting seeds of faith" is just as important as "harvesting the crop." I had to leave the results with God.

My own prayer life has never been the same. I *know* God hears the prayers of His people. I long to be like Mama—so "tuned in" to Him that He trusts me to pray for others who are in the middle of the battle. I wonder . . . when Mama's gone, who will stand in the gap?

*"I looked for a man among them who would build up the wall and stand before me in the gap on behalf of the land . . . but I found none."*
Ezekiel 22:30

*Ah, Yahweh, listen to my prayer, my cry— open your ears. Don't be callous; just look at these tears of mine.*
Psalm 39:12, MSG

# A Snapshot of Elisabeth Elliot

VALERIE ELLIOT SHEPARD

LIFE LESSON FROM MOTHER:
*You can confidently trust
your heavenly Father.*

One of my earliest jungle memories is canoeing up the river with several Auca men to watch them spear fish. As a curious five-year-old, I loved watching the dark water and seeing the sudden white flash of a fish come up on the ends of the men's spears.

*"Worry is the antithesis of trust. You simply
cannot do both. They are mutually
exclusive . . . Direct your time and energy
into worry, and you will be deficient in
things like singing with grace in your heart,
praying with thanksgiving, listening to a
child's account of his schoolday, inviting a
lonely person to supper, sitting down to talk
unhurriedly with wife or husband, writing
a note to someone who needs it."*

—ELISABETH ELLIOT, *THE GLAD SURRENDER*

I thoroughly enjoyed my life—schoolwork in the mornings with my mother, then afternoon play with the Indians. Yes, there were scorpions, boa constrictors, and wild boars that could have killed me, but I was never made aware of any anxiety on my mother's part. Looking back, I suppose many would think it was amazing that she gave me so much freedom to explore the jungle and play in the rivers, since my father had been speared to death by these same men only a few years earlier. But I realize now that my mother deeply trusted the Lord, and she completely entrusted her only child to God's capable hands.

My mother believed God brought us to the Aucas to share the good news with them. Every night when she put me to bed, she sang and prayed for us. I always felt completely secure and safe. I still remember two special songs from those childhood years in the jungle—"Jesus, Tender Shepherd, Hear Me" and "The Lord Is My Shepherd."

Perhaps the most important gift from my mother was that she instilled in me a confident trust in my heavenly Father. She believes and lives the promises of God.[1]

*The eternal God is your refuge,*
*and underneath are the everlasting arms.*
Deuteronomy 33:27

# The Fire
# and the Snowbank

NELLIE PICKARD

LIFE LESSON FROM MOTHER:
*God loves me and has a significant plan
for my future.*

"Fire! Fire! Your house is on fire!" our neighbor yelled.
"Everyone must get out of the house at once."

Mother opened her eyes and thought, *Who is at the
door? Why is someone waking us up in the middle of the
night?* In a flash, reality swept over her. *The house is on fire!*

Frantically she called upstairs to our live-in baby sitter:
"Ingrid, Ingrid, the house is on fire. You must get out of the
house at once!"

Ingrid dashed down the stairs and out the front door
crying, "It's in my room . . . the fire is in my room."

Mother noticed that Ingrid was alone. "Where is Nellie?"

"I'm sorry!" Ingrid wailed. "She's still upstairs!"

Without waiting to hear more, mother dashed into
the burning house and rescued me. Even though I was
only four years old at the time, I realized my mother had
risked her life for me.

Years later I was reminiscing about the fire, and my
mother said, "Nellie, do you realize that God spared your
life twice?"

"What do you mean?"

"Well, you may not remember, but when you were
two-and-a-half years old, you had the mumps. I went to

your room to check on you, but you weren't there. After searching all over the house, I called the neighbors and asked them to help me find you. You were so sick and had such a high fever—and I didn't know what could have happened to you.

*"The Bible teaches that 'God is love' and that God loves you. To realize that is of paramount importance. Nothing else matters so much. And loving you, God has wonderful plans for your life. Who else could plan and guide your life so well?"*

—BILLY GRAHAM, *GREAT QUOTES & ILLUSTRATIONS*

"Finally, we found you outside, asleep in a snowbank. You could have frozen to death, but God chose to save you. So, you see, Nellie, God chose to save you twice!"

"Yes, He did," I said. "Once from the fire and once from the ice."

My mother taught me that my life was precious to God and that He had something special in mind for my future.

*It's in Christ that we find out who we are and what we are living for. Long before we first heard of Christ and got our hopes up, He had His eye on us, had designs on us for glorious living, part of the overall purpose He is working out in everything and everyone.*
Ephesians 1:11-12, MSG

# Life-Changing Advice

NAOMI RHODE

LIFE LESSON FROM MOTHER:
*Love is a decision.*

I held my mother's hand, denying her words, "I am going to die today, and there are two things I must say to you before I leave."

Her hands and arms were so fragile. The white-gold wedding ring and filigreed diamond engagement ring moved loosely on her finger where they had worn thin after years of wearing.

*How could this be? She wouldn't die.* I was twenty-three years old with two tiny children, and the hope for at least one more. *What would I do without her?*

It was a bitterly cold day, even inside the hospital room. At twenty degrees below zero, the north wind blew giant icicles against the windowpane.

The attending physician examined her. He told me in hushed hospital talk that he felt she was perhaps a bit better, and there was no reason to think she would die today.

But she persisted with the same declaration: "I am going to die today. Please, Naomi, sit down where I can hold your hand and tell you what I must say before I leave.

"First, my precious Naomi, you have been given a wonderful husband. Jim will always protect and love you sacrificially. He will provide generously for you and instruct and raise your children after God's plan for families. He was given to you by a very special mother, Agnes. In pouring out your love to me, you have overlooked her. You have been gracious, polite, and hospitable to her, but you have not truly chosen to love her. I am asking you to *decide to love Agnes,* as the mother she is, the woman of God she is, and the schoolteacher that she is. To love her strengths and her weaknesses. Love like that is a decision. And I ask you to call her Mother.

*"Love is not only something you feel. It's something you do."*

—DAVID WILKERSON, *QUOTABLE QUOTES*

"Second, I want to hold you one more time and tell you that you have been the most wonderful daughter anyone could ever have. I am so proud of you and I love you so much."

Right at that moment she looked up and said, "The Lord be praised, the Lord be praised," and closed her eyes and died. For a moment I thought I heard the sound of trumpets.

In the weeks that followed, I wrestled with the decision to *choose* to love my mother-in-law, Agnes Katherine. My thoughts tumbled about. I thought of how different she was from my mother—more pragmatic, more "left-brained" and unemotional. I wondered what would happen if I truly decided to love her and call her Mother.

Months later Agnes came to help me with my new baby girl. I had named the baby Katherine Ellen, after my two precious mothers.

My mother's advice lingered in my heart. "*Decide* to love," she had said.

I will never forget the shocked and loving response I received the first time I humbly and with trembling voice called Agnes Katherine, "Mother." Her response was profound joy, love, and sacrificial giving.

The joy it brought to my own heart surprised me. I soon realized that deciding to love my husband's mother and family was a gift of honor, and a decision that comes with God's blessing and promise.

Agnes has lived in our guest house for the past sixteen years and has been a loyal, loving mother-in-law to me in every way.

My three children have grown up and now have children of their own—*eleven* grandchildren at last count!—and they cherish their own mothers-in-law.

Today, as I hold my mother's thin white-gold wedding rings, I know they are a symbol of the legacy of love she gave to me that will be passed on to the next generation.

*That precious memory triggers another:*
*your honest faith—and what a rich faith it is,*
*handed down from your grandmother Lois*
*to your mother Eunice, and now to you!*
2 Timothy 1:5, MSG

# The Attack

ANNE DENMARK

LIFE LESSON FROM MOTHER:
*Modeling the compassion of Christ will
change the hearts of your children.*

Something was wrong. My husband always followed a
routine when he came home for lunch. He would take off
his coat at the door and then call, "Hi Honey! I'm home."
Today was different.

With his coat still on, Don climbed the front stairs and
found me. I read the expression on his face and knew he
had something difficult to tell me. He came closer and
placed his hands on my shoulders. My heart began to
pound.

"Honey, I just received a phone call from your dad.
It's about your mother. She was physically beaten—by a
young man—in her office—early this morning."

My tangled thoughts were filled with shock and dis-
belief. *Mom. Beaten? Who would want to hurt my mother?*

"Anne, she's going to be okay. An ambulance took her
to the hospital. Her head is badly cut and bruised, but her
condition is not critical. She will be okay."

My stomach writhed with a nauseating anger. *How
dare anyone strike my mother? How could anyone hurt
such a soft-spoken woman?* I wanted to hit back. I wanted
someone to hurt for this injustice.

While my husband drove me to the hospital, I prayed,
asking God to help me make some sense out of this event.
We entered her room, and I was startled to realize the

form on the bed was my precious mother.

Her face was swollen and discolored from the internal bruising, and I could hardly visualize her fine cheekbones. The whites of her eyes were red with blood. Her soft blond hair had been shaved off and tight rows of black stitches stretched far across her scalp and down her forehead. She could barely move her head, but she wanted to tell us the story.

*"A guard at Ravensbruck who was later converted to Christ went to hear Corrie (ten Boom) speak . . . After the meeting he went up and said, ' . . . Do you recognize me?' As she looked at him, she realized he was one of the guards who had been so brutal and unmerciful to her and (her sister) Betsie. He said, 'I have come to ask your forgiveness.'*

*Later Corrie said, 'In myself, I could not. But then I remembered what Jesus Christ did for me upon the cross. And I called upon His divine love, and I felt it coming into my heart. And I looked at him, and said, In my strength, I cannot. But in Jesus' strength, I can. Yes my brother, I do forgive.'"*

—CORRIE TEN BOOM, *CLIPPINGS FROM MY NOTEBOOK*

Mom, a travel agent, had arrived at her office around 8:30 A.M. to open the door for early deliveries. A young man, about fifteen years old, came in to purchase a bus ticket. She began writing out the ticket when she heard him pull something from his jacket. As she looked up, the boy struck her on the forehead with a marble pestle, a tool used to force meat into a grinder. She later discovered he had taken it from his father's meat market at the local grocery store. The boy began beating her over the head repeatedly while she fought for her life.

Although Mom was in excellent physical shape and she exercised regularly, her clawing and kicking did little to ward off the continual blows from her attacker. Suddenly, she recalled a tactic from an article she had read on self-defense.

Calling out the name of a coworker, she screamed, "Jackie! Please come and help me! Come quickly!" In the panic and confusion of the moment, the young man forgot they were alone and ran for the door. Mom crawled out of the office to the road, pleading for someone to help her.

What happened next was a miracle. Even before the ambulance arrived, the attacker confessed his crime to his father. The boy's father immediately returned to the scene and rushed to offer assistance to my mother. He said, "I am so sorry!"

Incredulously, I listened as mother said she looked into the man's eyes, saw his pain, and said, "I am so sorry for you, too."

In my humanness, I imagined the many angry and bitter things my mother could have said. *Things that I was feeling.* Mother continued, "I really meant it, Anne. In that instant I felt that father's pain."

My mother's response to the father of her attacker has forever changed my life. In the midst of her own terror and personal pain, she felt the need of someone else and demonstrated compassion—the compassion of Jesus Christ.

*This is the kind of life you've been invited into,*
*the kind of life Christ lived. He suffered everything*
*that came his way so you would know*
*that it could be done, and also know how to do it,*
*step by step. "He never did one thing wrong,*
*Not once said anything amiss." They called Him*
*every name in the book and He said nothing back.*
*He suffered in silence, content to let God set things right.*
1 Peter 2:21-23, MSG

*Jesus prayed, "Father, forgive them;*
*they don't know what they're doing."*
Luke 23:34, MSG

# Let the Fog Roll In!

CAROL JOHN

LIFE LESSON FROM MOTHER:
*Faithful love is a precious gift
to pass on to others.*

One week after I was born the headlines in the newspaper announced my condition: TINY INFANT STRICKEN WITH POLIO. It was the summer of 1952, six months before the Salk polio vaccine was first tested, and California was experiencing one of the worst polio epidemics in recent history. My mother was nine months pregnant when she came down with polio. But because polio has an incubation period, no one knew we both had polio until a week after I was born.

Mom was only twenty-five years old. My sister, Diane, was two and a half. During the next six weeks there were many changes in the family's day-to-day routine. My father was driving to Los Angeles every day to attend graduate school, so my grandma came out from Wisconsin by train to help care for us.

Six weeks later, Mom had fully recovered, but I was completely paralyzed from head to toe. I could only open and close one eye and move one finger. I could do nothing on my own.

As the years went by and the reality of a severe disability was an obvious part of my daily life, I came face to face with the truth of Psalm 139:15-16:

> My frame was not hidden from you when I was
> made in the secret place. When I was woven

together in the depths of the earth, your eyes saw my unformed body. *All the days ordained for me were written in your book before one of them came to be.* (emphasis added)

My "ordained days" included a loving, caring, and faithful set of parents and sisters. Even though my parents had their hands full with a five-year-old daughter and a two-and-a-half-year-old handicapped daughter, Mom and Dad had one more child, Susan. Sandwiched safely and securely between Diane and Suz, I was raised with a great deal of love and normalcy.

*"What does love look like?*
*It has the hands to help others.*
*It has the feet to hasten to the poor*
*and needy. It has eyes to see misery*
*and want. It has the ears*
*to hear the sighs and sorrows of men.*
*That is what love looks like."*

—AUGUSTINE, *QUOTABLE QUOTATIONS*

Despite the physical care I needed, the three of us were emotionally cared for equally. There were *no* favorites. In fact, one Christmas when the three of us sisters were in our twenties, we were all talking when Diane responded to a casual remark, half jokingly, that *she* was the favorite child. Suz immediately responded that *she*, in fact, was the favorite. I chimed in right away that they were both wrong, because I *knew* that *I* was the favorite! Mom and Dad just grinned at each other.

I was seven years old before mother ever left me alone with a neighbor for the day. Throughout my elementary years she delivered me to school and picked me up. And every day she came to school at noon to take me to the bathroom. Years later, when I began attending college, she again came to school with me daily, to lift my electric wheelchair from the trunk of the car and assemble it. It was four years later when the first vans with lifts were available. Mom says: "The first day Carol drove off to begin work on her master's degree in her new van was as emotionally difficult for me as her first day of kindergarten."

At the age of ten I had a spinal fusion and spent ten months in a body cast. The heavy cast began behind my head, continued under my chin, and went over my shoulders and down past my waist to my hips. In order for me to sleep comfortably, a piece of plywood was placed under my sheet to keep me from sinking into the bed, and the weight of the cast made it impossible for me to turn myself over.

Dad designed the house we lived in and built an intercom system between our bedrooms. Mom kept the intercom tuned in to my room every night. Early each morning, if I needed to be turned over, I called to Mom with a low, two-toned "Maaa—ahhmm." She would get up, shuffle down the hall half-asleep, turn me over, and go back to bed.

One morning I woke to realize I was being turned over, but I hadn't called her. Later that morning I told her I hadn't called. But she was convinced she'd heard my unmistakable two-toned call. Suddenly, we heard it again:

"Mmmm—mmmmm!" We looked at each other and laughed out loud. It was the foghorn blowing along the shore three miles away.

A month later I found myself being turned over again without having called. I will never forget the unshakable and certain feeling of love that I had that morning as I thought, "Hmmmm, it must be foggy today." My mother's tangible devotion is a continuing reflection of God's faithful and unwavering love.

*But I trust in your unfailing love;*
*my heart rejoices in your salvation.*
*I will sing to the LORD, for he has been good to me.*
Psalm 13:5-6

*This is how we've come to understand*
*and experience love: Christ sacrificed his life for us. . . .*
*My dear children, let's not just talk about love;*
*let's practice real love.*
1 John 3:16,18; MSG

# Life Is a Pressure Cooker!

BETTY SOUTHARD

LIFE LESSON FROM GRANDMA:
*Step back and release the pressure
before you blow your top!*

Grandma loved to cook. Her fantastic dishes were never-fail recipes. Well, most of the time! When I was a little girl, my grandparents lived with us for a while, and sometimes I got to help Grandma in the kitchen.

*"Nobody can do for little children
what grandparents do. Grandparents
sort of sprinkle stardust over the lives
of little children."*

—ALEX HALEY, QUOTED IN *A RAINBOW OF HOPE*

One day we drove to Aunt Mabel's apple orchard and gathered baskets of apples. The following day we spent hours and hours peeling and slicing the fruit we had gathered. Grandma made some of the apples into pies. Others were stored in the family freezer for future enjoyment. But my personal favorite was Grandma's special homemade applesauce. Its spicy scent titillated my nose and engaged my salivary glands.

To prepare this delicacy Grandma hauled out an

intimidating pot with a funny dial on top—*the pressure cooker!* It was late in the afternoon when the apples went into the cooker. The kitchen was a cluttered mess—with apple peelings, cores, sugar, flour, and spices everywhere. The men would be coming home for dinner soon and no one had even started to think of what we would eat. We were hot and tired. Our nerves were frayed.

Suddenly, without warning, the pressure cooker exploded. Applesauce spewed everywhere—on the walls, the floor, dripping off the ceiling. For an instant we were speechless. Then Grandma came to her senses and shooed me toward the kitchen door, away from the hot applesauce. She bravely grabbed the pot and released the pressure, only to have more applesauce spit out.

Without warning Grandma began to laugh. Not a little chuckle, but a deep, rippling belly laugh that went from the top of her head to the bottom of her feet. As I looked around at our hopeless situation, I started laughing, too. The kitchen was a mess. *We* were a mess. That day, in the middle of chaos, we laughed until we cried.

*"Life is full of bumps, potholes,
and even washed-out bridges.
So we need all the shock absorbers
we can get! More doctors are agreeing
that everyone needs to laugh more."*

—Barbara Johnson, *Mama, Get the Hammer*

That day Grandma taught me a lesson for a lifetime. Often, my life feels like a pressure cooker. There isn't enough time for all I have to do. There isn't enough money to go around. Demands, expectations, and obligations press in on all sides. The pressure builds until my "pot" is on the verge of spewing out a mess on those I love. That's when I need to pause, assess the situation, and look for the humor in it.

By the way, we did get that awful mess cleaned up. After a simple dinner, with applesauce surrounding us, we divided the chores—and laughed out loud until the job was done.

*A happy heart is good medicine,*
*but a broken spirit drains your strength.*
Proverbs 17:22, NCV

# Mother's Hospitality

NANCY GROOM

LIFE LESSON FROM MOTHER:
*Opening your heart and home to refresh
others reflects the very character of God.*

I returned home from the airport that stifling July afternoon and slumped gratefully into the nearest chair. My house was disheveled but blessedly quiet, though already I missed our friends. My husband, Bill, put words to the moment: "It's good to have our house back," he said, "but it's a bittersweet 'good.'"

He was right. For two weeks we had opened our modest home to five extra people. With some creative rearranging and the advantage of pool and patio, we'd somehow managed to find the physical and personal space for genuinely enjoying our guests, especially our three "adopted grandchildren." Nonetheless, the silence greeting us after their departure was, for the moment at least, golden.

*Why do I keep doing this?* I wondered to myself wearily, thinking back to other friends who had visited two months earlier and the flurry of family I'd entertained the Christmas before that. Why do I disrupt my life and my house, only to spend two weeks recovering my equilibrium and putting my guest room/office back to rights again? What possesses me to repeat this craziness?

Then I remembered the phone call. Two weeks before Christmas, three days before my parents were to leave their Michigan home to visit us in Miami, I had called to check out final details with my seventy-nine-year-old mother.

74

"Are you all packed and ready to come?" I asked cheerily.

"Well, not quite," my mother admitted. "I talked to Uncle Ernie yesterday, and he said your cousin Janice and her four children are coming here to visit him for Christmas. They planned to stay in a motel for the week, but I told him they're welcome to stay at our house while we're gone. Right now I'm straightening things up and getting some food ready for them."

*"When you thought I wasn't looking, I saw you make my favorite cake just for me, and I knew that little things are special things."*

—AUTHOR UNKNOWN

"If that isn't just like you, Mother!" I said with a laugh, shaking my head. "You've always opened your home to those who need it—it's one reason I love you so much. But I hope you're saving enough energy for your visit here."

When we got off the phone, I reflected fondly on my mother's typical kindness. All my life I'd observed her working overtime to provide pleasant experiences to delight and refresh others.

I recalled the innumerable parties she'd hosted for us children and our friends; the spontaneous coffee breaks with fresh-baked goodies she was always offering our neighbors; the year-after-year holiday celebrations she'd orchestrated for us and our extended family; not to mention the countless Sunday meals she prepared for people at church—people she knew and those she didn't know. And the overnight guests in her home—how many had there been over the decades? Certainly hundreds have tasted my mother's wonderful food and experienced her generous heart. Why should I have been surprised that before leaving for her Florida Christmas she would try to make a Michigan Christmas "homey" for my cousin and her family?

And why should I be surprised that I, too, enjoy opening my home to those I love and who need my care? *Maybe hospitality is in my genes,* I thought.

More likely, I have learned to share my heart and my house by having seen my mother's kindness oft repeated with no thought of repayment. She and my father will surely recognize more than a few angels when they get Home, for they have welcomed many a stranger, many a time.

Despite my post-visit weariness that summer day, I found myself hoping my children could someday say the same about me. That they would see a lifestyle reflecting the benevolent heart of my heavenly Father, exemplified in the life of my earthly mother, and perpetuate it themselves as a family tradition—even when it ushers in the inevitable ambivalence of a now-too-quiet house.

*Be ready with a meal or a bed when it's needed.*
*Why, some have extended hospitality to angels*
*without ever knowing it!*
Hebrews 13:2, MSG

# Pretty Is As Pretty Does

LINDSEY O'CONNOR

LIFE LESSON FROM MOTHER:
*Beauty stems from internal character,
reflected in the external.*

I was six years old and I had a problem. I was wearing my
favorite dress, a vivid pink knit jumper with gold buttons,
and I was miserable.

"What color is my dress again, Mommy?" I asked.

"Hot pink," she replied.

"Boy, that's for sure. It's the hottest thing I ever wore!"

I was clueless as to why my parents suddenly burst
out laughing. What in the world was so funny about me
sweltering in my hot pink dress? They certainly had the
name of the color right. But my real problem was deciding if being this hot was a price I was willing to pay for
looking so great. You see, I looked stunning in that dress.
At least that's what *I* thought.

I explained my "suffering for the price of beauty"
dilemma to my mother. I expected her to offer soothing
words of comfort and advice. Instead she uttered five
words I was to hear often over the next decade and a half:
"Pretty is as pretty does." She explained that looking good
on the outside isn't nearly as important as *being* good.
Funny thing. I don't remember the *hot* pink dress being
much of a problem after that.

When I hit my preteen years I battled some of the same
monsters many adolescents face. My stunning appearance
never even crossed my mind now. Knobby knees did. I don't

remember talking with Mother about this. She just knew. Suddenly "pretty is as pretty does" began to take on a new slant. Now when she said it, she meant: "Don't compare yourself to those other girls. You may think they're prettier than you are, but remember—pretty is as pretty does." Then she began to build my self-image by focusing on the good aspects of my character and actions.

*"If a woman understands who she is in divine perspective, she can move herself into her rightful position of royalty by allowing God to take charge of her life . . . Her preference for prettiness will be crushed unless a woman allows the Lord Himself to open her eyes to see His version of beauty."*

—JEANNE HENDRICKS, WOMEN OF HONOR

When I was six, the expression meant: "You watch how you act, Missy. Don't think you're so hot. It's more important to *act* right." In junior high it meant: "You watch how those other girls act. You may think they look pretty, but their character may not be up to snuff, and that's what's important."

When I was in high school Mother noticed I needed both reminders.

There were some days when I had more than enough self-confidence for everyone in Typing 101. After all, I just knew those platform shoes made me look great! Platform shoes made everyone walk a little funny, but when Mother noticed my gait had an unusual saunter accompanied by a sassy flip of the hair, she gently reined me in with, "Pretty is . . ." It became a family expression we all completed in unison, but Mother remained undaunted. The implied message was clear.

Then came the high school days when I had enough self-*doubt* for everyone in Typing 101, 201, and the fourth period P. E. class, and my self-worth hinged on being able to do the splits for drill team tryouts. The other girls could jump up in the air and land in the splits like graceful ballerinas. The closest I came to the splits was Dairy Queen's bananas and whipped cream. I got cut early in the tryouts and came home to wallow in my misery with a good cry and some chocolate chip cookies. I told my mom that I could never face those beautiful and talented girls again. But like the refrain of a familiar and comforting song I heard, "Yes, but pretty is as pretty does."

Amidst my teenage tears the true meaning of that phrase built me up. Mother's words became the balance that always brought me back to center during those years, a challenge to godly character. Her witticism taught me to remember not to be obnoxious (a handy tip), and the fact that worth and beauty come from internal character, not external things like looks or accomplishments.

*What matters is not your outer appearance—*
*the styling of your hair, the jewelry you wear,*
*the cut of your clothes—but your inner disposition.*
*Cultivate inner beauty, the gentle, gracious kind*
*that God delights in.*
1 Peter 3:3-4, MSG

# My Conscience, My Compass

Laurie McIntyre

LIFE LESSON FROM MOTHER:
*A dimmed conscience is a broken compass.*

My mother was constantly about the business of tending to my conscience. It was her conviction that a well-developed conscience was the key to my discerning right from wrong, better from best, and God's ways from man's ways. And so it was that life and all its venues were regularly evaluated for their values. Such conversations could happen anywhere— at the dinner table, in the car, at the mall, on the school bleachers, on a walk, in front of the television, and even in the bathroom! But the most noteworthy occasion was in the parking lot of a movie theater.

As an impressionable thirteen year old, I had just swooned over John Travolta's baby blues and boyish grin, and crooned with Olivia Newton John's heartbreaking ballads in the teen craze *Grease*—the big screen version! Do you remember the plot? Danny was a black-leathered greaser and Sandy an innocent in a poodle-skirt. They had fallen in love over summer vacation, neither knowing the other's true identity until she showed up as the new girl in town at his school! Unfortunately "summer love" faded into autumn's heartbreak until Danny decided to shed his greaser image and become the proverbial good guy jock.

He failed miserably, albeit humorously, leaving Sandy soulfully singing, "Hopelessly devoted to you . . ." As in classic fifties flicks, the plot climbs toward the inevitable drag race on the far side of town, and Sandy decides how to get her man.

Young female audience members were poised in feverish anticipation as Sandy finally appeared, stepping over a cement barricade dressed in sexy, skin-tight, black leather, spike heels, with painted lips, big hair, and a "Virginia Slim" balanced delicately between perfectly manicured red-hot nails. Not one teenager will forget the way she vanquished the glowing embers with just a touch of her toe. Danny didn't stand a chance. Everyone, *except my mother,* fairly exploded when he swept her into his arms!

*"'Oh, yes,' said the Indian,*
*'I know what my conscience is.*
*It is a little three-cornered thing in here'—*
*he laid his hand on his heart—*
*'that stands still when I'm good;*
*but when I am bad it turns around,*
*and the corners hurt very much.*
*But if I keep on doing wrong,*
*by and by the corners wear off*
*and it doesn't hurt anymore.'"*

—Anonymous, *Quotable Quotations*

Believing that true love had conquered, I floated out of my seat, down the aisle, and into the back seat of the car. I was dreaming of the boy who would one day love me that much when my mother interrupted my fantasy with the words, "What do you think was wrong with that movie?"

*Wrong?* I thought. Nothing. It was perfect in every way, and I wished Mom would go away. But she insisted on a reality and morality check. Mom asked probing questions about what Sandy had to do to win the boy of her dreams.

Mom could have easily left me to my back-seat reveries and chalked it up to a harmless romance. But instead, she tended to my impressionable conscience. She helped me discern the subtleties of sin in the hope that I would some-day recognize compromises in my own life.

I learned from Mom that my conscience is my compass; without it I am destined for shipwreck.

> *Holding on to faith and a good conscience.*
> *Some have rejected these and so*
> *have shipwrecked their faith.*
> 1 Timothy 1:19

# Living Life Abundantly

CAROLYN LUNN

LIFE LESSON FROM MOTHER:
*God enables us to face life's challenges with
faith and persevering love.*

The late summer sun slanted across our deck, casting soft
shadows through the large glass door in our kitchen. The
table, set for four, was filled with food. I wanted it to be
special because Mom and Dad were visiting from Texas. I
invited them to the table and watched as Mother tried to
negotiate this simple procedure. It was difficult for her. She
was five feet ten inches tall and couldn't bring her long legs
under the table. When she finally did, she turned and gave
me the most irrepressible smile, as if to say, "Look! I did it!"

I was shocked into awareness of how serious Mother's
condition was. My father had conveyed the facts of her
memory loss and deterioration of coordination and manual
skills, but I didn't realize her Alzheimer's was progressing
so rapidly.

My mother was an elegant lady. By nature she was
quiet and shy, but she had a delightful sense of humor.
However, she said very little that night, seemingly content to listen to the conversation. Later, my father asked
if we had noticed how little she spoke during dinner.
Then he explained that she didn't talk much anymore
because she was aware of her illness and didn't want to
repeat stories over and over again. She had always
demonstrated such sweet dignity. I understood she didn't
want to be embarrassed.

Because of mother's illness, my parents were moving to our city where they could be near my sister and me. The next afternoon, my husband and my father went to look once again at a house my dad had decided to buy. While they were gone, Mother sat in a chair, leafing through a magazine. She turned a few pages, briefly looking at the pictures and put it down. I knew she could not comprehend what she was reading. Suddenly she stood to her feet and started to walk toward the door. She turned to me with a puzzled look on her face and said, "Where is my husband?"

"Mother, he went to look at your new house again. He'll be home soon." At that moment we heard the garage door going up. Mother went to the kitchen doorway and looked toward the back hall. When the door opened and my father walked into the kitchen, she stared at him intently for a moment. Then she walked over to him quickly, threw her arms around him, and kissed him passionately!

As she finished, Dad (with a flush on his face) said, "*My,* what did I do to deserve *that?*"

My mother impishly laughed and said, "I call them like I see them. When I recognize him, I kiss him!" We all laughed delightedly. She had not lost her sense of humor!

The next day Mother tried to talk to me about what was happening to her. An accomplished musician, she shared her pain over losing the ability to play her violin. She had been able to play almost any song she heard. Her music had been a source of pleasure and comfort for years, but now she was afraid to play in public.

I reached across to comfort her as the tears slipped down her face. She said, "My friend, Naomi, told me to keep on practicing, to hold on to my music. So I'm going upstairs to my room now to practice. I'm determined to play as long as I can."

Slowly and laboriously we climbed the stairs to her room. As I prepared the evening meal, I could hear her tune up her violin and then she began to play. She kept playing a song over and over. I knew she was having trouble remembering the music, but she didn't give up. She kept going over and over it until she remembered a little more. In former days her music had been smooth and melodic. Now her lack of dexterity made the bow screech and the notes were not quite true.

*"How do I manage a difficulty? Well, at first I try to walk past it. If that does not help, I try to climb over it; and when I cannot climb over it, to crawl underneath. And when that is not possible I go straight through—God and I!"*

—CORRIE TEN BOOM, *CLIPPINGS FROM MY NOTEBOOK*

It was more than I could handle. My mother's violin playing was one of the sweetest memories I had of my childhood. Tears rolled down my face as I listened to her. *What a gutsy lady! I thought. Most people would have given up—but she's determined to be a part of life as long as she can!*

Mother had always lived that way. As a result of my birth and complications afterwards, mother had a blood circulatory condition in her legs. She often suffered with ulcers on her ankles because of poor circulation and needed almost complete bed rest until the ulcer healed—each time. *Never once* during my growing-up years did I hear my mother complain. She never blamed me for her troubles by saying, "If it hadn't been for your birth, I would be well!" I didn't even know it was my birth that caused her health problem until I was in my teen years.

Two weeks before Mother died, I was sitting beside her bed, holding her hand. She turned her head in my direction and gave me her beautiful smile and said, "Oh-h-h!" She had not known who I was before that moment, but in that instant, she knew me.

I stood up beside the bed and leaned over to take her sweet face between my hands and said, "Mother, I love you so much. You are the best mother a girl could ever have. I want you to know that you are the most significant person in my life! You nurtured me in my faith and in my personhood. I don't know what would have happened to me without you! Thank you, Mother, for being you!"

The only way she could respond was with her radiant smile. The tears began to flow down her face and I knew she understood me. But in an instant she was gone, back into that mind-numbing world. I'd had only a few moments, but I had been given a priceless gift—the chance to say thank you to a loving, wise mother for a life lived *abundantly!*

*I came so they can have real and eternal life,*
*more and better life than they ever dreamed of.*
John 10:10, MSG

# A Wise Maneuver

CAROLE MAYHALL

LIFE LESSON FROM MOTHER:
*Those who sit in God's presence
will receive His wisdom.*

"Carole, I'm not going to tell you not to smoke." Mother's brown eyes looked serious as I glanced at her in surprise. A few of my girlfriends had begun to experiment with smoking "behind the barn," and Mother and I were discussing it. I knew my parents disapproved of smoking, so I was quite shocked by her initial statement.

She continued, "I cannot be either your judge or your keeper as you are growing up, so I'm not going to tell you that you must not smoke." She paused and then said, "But I *am* going to ask you to promise me that you will smoke your first cigarette *in front of me*."

In our household, a promise was not given lightly. It had the solemnity of a sacred oath sworn on the Bible. To my knowledge my parents had never broken a promise to me and we were expected to act just as honorably.

A wise woman, my mother. I didn't know it when I promised that day, but she had just taken all the wicked fun out of sneaking off somewhere to smoke with friends. To this day I have never had a cigarette in my lips, because who in her right mind would smoke her first in front of a mother she loved and respected, and whom she knew would be heartbroken to witness the event? Definitely not this kid!

I learned early that Mother gained her wisdom from

God. Often I'd see her coming out of her room with tears drying on her cheeks, and I knew Mom had been sitting at the feet of the Lord Jesus, who is Wisdom, listening to Him and praying for her family and others. As my years increase, my appreciation of Mother's godly qualities increases even more, and I seek to emulate her.

*"Our kids need our acceptance and attention, enough attention that we pick up on what hurts, intimidates, and tempts them."*

—LINDA WEBER, *MOM, YOU'RE INCREDIBLE*

And Mom, I hope you know from where you are on the Other Side: I've had to deal with a lot of issues in my life, but thanks to you, smoking has not been one of them!

*Parents rejoice when their children turn out well;*
*wise children become proud parents.*
Proverbs 23:24, MSG

# The Leftover Doll

LUCINDA SECREST MCDOWELL

LIFE LESSON FROM MOTHER:
*Love understands and extends grace.*

"What do you mean you don't want a doll for Christmas?" Mama asked. "You've been talking of nothing else for months, Cindy!"

"Well . . . I don't," I stated. "Everybody gets a doll for Christmas, and I don't *want* to be like everybody else!"

Mama looked at me standing there with arms crossed and chest out. She lowered her voice to a gentle pleading, "Cindy, are you *sure?*"

"I am, Mama, really I am. I'm seven years old and I really don't need a doll," I said, trying to sound grown up.

Weeks passed with the usual holiday hubbub of pageants, parties, and present-wrapping. Finally, the long-awaited moment arrived—Christmas morning!

My sisters and I knew we had to stay at the top of the staircase until Mama and Daddy came to get us, so we got as close as we could and peered into the shadows of the living room at the mysterious bundles that flanked the central fireplace.

Santa left our gifts in the same place each year: Cathy's to the left of the fireplace in the big wing chair, Susan's to the right of the fireplace in the love seat, and mine (because I was, after all, the middle child) right in the middle—front and center!

"Merry Christmas! Everybody up!" boomed my daddy's

laughing voice. No matter that we'd been up for hours. Whenever he awakened, the word was, "Everybody up!"

"Hmmmm . . . looks like Santa must have been here— all he left are cookie crumbs and an empty milk glass," Daddy said with a chuckle.

"Surely that isn't *all* he's left, Daddy?" four-year-old Susan softly inquired, her big blue eyes wide. She not only looked like an angel, she acted like one.

"Don't be silly!" Cathy said, worldly wise at age ten. She had Santa pretty well figured out. "Oooh, I can't believe it! He brought me a *Poor Pitiful Pearl doll!*"

I stopped to gaze at what was perhaps the ugliest doll I had ever seen. Fortunately, Poor Pitiful Pearl was a somewhat short-lived success, designed to play on the pity and compassion of young girls. Nonetheless, Cathy had wanted her and Cathy had gotten her.

"Mama, look—it's *Thumbelina!*" was all Susan could say as she cradled the soft baby doll in her arms, cooing and clucking just as Mama had done to her not so long ago. Thumbelina Secrest was clearly the new baby of our family.

I focused on my own pile of gifts. To this day, I don't remember what Santa brought. My only memories are of what was so obviously missing—a doll.

My secret disappointment did not spoil Christmas Day, nor our family gathering. I always looked forward to the annual tape-recording session with Daddy when he interviewed us and we got to perform whatever songs or poetry or Bible verses we had learned that year. Perry Como, Frank Sinatra, and Judy Garland serenaded us with Christmas favorites on the hi-fi, and all was cozy.

I was almost too sleepy to talk with my friend, Cax, when she called, reminding me of our new tradition of sharing the day after Christmas together.

"Oh, and don't forget to bring your new doll." Cax said, and hung up before I could tell her I didn't have a new doll.

The next day Mama helped me pack my overnight things. "Cindy, was it kind of hard not getting a doll when your sisters both got one?" she asked.

"Not at all!" I said, a bit too cheerily. "I had a great Christmas, Mama."

*"Grace is the active expression of His love. The Christian lives by grace as Abba's child, utterly rejecting the God who catches people by surprise in a sign of weakness . . . This is the God of the gospel of grace. A God, who out of love for us, sent the only Son he ever had wrapped in our skin. He learned how to walk, stumbled and fell, cried for his milk, sweated blood in the night, was lashed with a whip and showered with spit, was fixed to a cross and died whispering forgiveness on us all."*

—BRENNAN MANNING, *THE RAGAMUFFIN GOSPEL*

But this wise woman, all of thirty-three, could read me like a book. I've always worn my heart on my sleeve, and on the way to Cax's house, it broke open.

"Mama!" I cried, "I *did* want a doll but I just didn't *know* I wanted one so I told you I *didn't* want one, but I knew you would *know* that I really *did,* but instead you believed me and so I didn't *get* a doll but now I *want* one and I'm going to Cax's to play dolls but I don't *have* one and I know this makes me seem ungrateful 'cause I had such a nice Christmas, but Mama . . ."

"Yes, Cindy?"

"I really *did* want a doll."

"I see," she said.

I know now that even though she was frustrated, her heart was probably breaking and she was praying like crazy for God's guidance. I know that now, because I, too, have a seven-year-old daughter who is named for my mother, but who acts just like me.

"Cindy?"

"Yes, Mama?"

"How many times have I *told* you that actions have consequences? If you go around declaring to the world that you don't want a doll for Christmas, then you shouldn't be surprised when you don't get one!"

"Yes, Ma'am."

Mama's "actions-have-consequences" sermon had hit home. But today I learned that my mother longed to give me good gifts. She looked at me and smiled.

"Cindygirl, let's go find a doll!"

Now, back in the sixties, small-town Georgia didn't have such things as giant toy stores or discount marts. We were your basic two-block downtown with small department stores at either end and one in the middle. And the stock of dolls was usually depleted long before Christmas.

Our chances of finding a doll were slim, but our hearts were high as we trudged from one store to another. After striking out twice, we were met at the final counter by a sympathetic clerk who peered down at me.

"Why, yes, honey, I do have one doll left, but I don't think you'll want her. Still . . . it's a shame nobody took her home for Christmas."

She walked into the back room and returned with a hard plastic doll with curly red hair and brown eyes. I could easily see why this doll had been passed over for the more popular soft-skinned, blond, blue-eyed babies. But what a *perfect* doll for someone like me who always liked to be just a little different!

Mama's eyes met mine. She instinctively knew that this doll was the one that would bring me true Christmas joy, all the more precious because I didn't deserve her.

"Mama, I love her already. Thank you so much—you're the bestest mama in the whole wide world!" I gushed, as we walked to the station wagon. "But what shall I name her?"

Without skipping a beat, Mama replied, "Joy. Why don't you call her *Joy?*"

It was a prophetic name. From that first sleepover at Cax's, Joy Secrest accompanied me everywhere. I kept a baby book documenting her family tree, first words, favorite foods, and birthday, December 26, 1960. She even wore my hand-me-down baby clothes. And she appears in almost all of my childhood photographs.

*"The grace of God is love freely shown
towards guilty sinners, contrary to their
merit . . . It is God showing goodness to
persons who deserve only severity."*

—J. I. Packer, *Knowing God*

Thirty-six years later, Joy and all her belongings are comfortably ensconced in my memory trunk down in our basement. She survived my childhood, but suffered a few breaks during visits with my own children.

Joy was always more than a doll to me. She was a symbol of my mother's love—a love that understood my childish immaturity and extended grace to me.

*But because God was so gracious,*
*so very generous,*
*here I am. And I'm not about*
*to let his grace go to waste.*
1 Corinthians 15:10, MSG

*What we've learned is this:*
*God does not respond to what we do;*
*we respond to what God does.*
Romans 3:27, MSG

# A Snapshot of Jill Briscoe

DR. JUDY BRISCOE GOLZ

LIFE LESSON FROM MOTHER:
*The ground between my own two feet
is holy ground.*

My mother was baking in the kitchen while I played in the living room with my toys. I had been hearing a lot about Jesus in my Sunday school class, and I knew with the limited knowledge of a four-year-old that to invite Him into my heart would mean that some things would have to change.

I approached my mother in the kitchen and asked, "If I invite Jesus into my heart, does that mean I'll have to put away all of my toys when you ask me to?"

"Yes," my mother said, "Jesus would want you to obey and put them away."

I thought about it for a few seconds and said, "Okay, then, I guess I won't," and walked away. A few minutes later I came back and said, "Even if I have to put away the toys, I want Jesus in my heart."

Without even wiping the flour off her hands, she went to the couch in our living room and knelt with me as I prayed to accept Jesus as my personal Savior.

Mom has since admitted to me that she struggled with how to answer my question about the toys. Everything in her mother-heart wanted me to invite Jesus into my heart and *then* deal with the questions and issues of the Christian life. Yet she knew that wouldn't honestly represent what Christ expected of me.

When I told her I wouldn't invite Jesus in and I walked

away, she let me go and entrusted me to Him. Now that I'm a mother, I know how difficult that must have been for her.

Mom has taught me that sometimes doing something or saying something may be the worst thing to do in a given situation. Instead, we need to pray that the Lord will guide us in relation to the other person and ask that His will be done.

*"Looking back over the influences on my life, the spiritual inheritance my mother gave her children stands out in memory."*

—A. WETHERELL JOHNSON, FOUNDER OF THE BIBLE STUDY FELLOWSHIP, *CREATED FOR COMMITMENT*

My mother also taught me that the ground between her own two feet was holy ground. At the time I asked her about Jesus, she was running a nursery school, working with street kids, and raising my brothers and me. Nonetheless, she knew that day that her main mission was to explain God's truth to me.

Now that I'm a mom, this lesson is especially relevant. Sometimes amidst the never-ending laundry and housecleaning, I forget that the ground between my feet is holy. God has placed me here for a purpose. I need to be His servant and minister to my children.[1]

*God said, "Kneel and pray.*
*You are in a holy place,*
*on holy ground."*
Acts 7:33, MSG

# High Button Shoes

MARGARET JENSEN

LIFE LESSON FROM MOTHER:
*Every day I have the power to choose
an attitude of thankfulness.*

I clutched the gift certificate in my hand and entered the fashionable shoe salon to purchase the most expensive shoes I had ever owned. A half hour later, I left the store clutching a gold-braided handle, swinging the precious purchase in its exquisite bag.

*These shoes will be perfect with my new outfit,* I thought. With a light step, I hurried to the parking lot and happened to pass a shoe repair shop with a pair of high button shoes in the window. The sight brought a flood of memories.

I heard my Norwegian mama's voice ring in my ears. "Oh, ja, Margaret, pride is a terrible thing. Wear your shoes with a thankful and a humble heart. This could be one of life's valuable lessons."

Tears welled up as I remembered being ten years old and watching my papa empty a missionary barrel packed with moth-eaten coats, hats with plumes and feathers, and corsets.

Then Papa reached to the bottom of the barrel and like a prophet of old, shouted, "Look, Margaret. God answered our prayers. *We have shoes!*" He held up two pairs of high button shoes, complete with the button hook.

I looked at those monstrosities and cried, "Oh, Papa, they are too big!" (Oxfords were "in." Button shoes were "out.")

My resourceful father quickly responded, "Oh, ja, that is good. We put cotton in the toes. They will last a long time."

No one answered Papa back. I stood in mute despair. Mama looked at me and then at the shoes.

"Margaret," she said gently, "we prayed for shoes. Now we have shoes. The Canadian winters are cold; the snow is deep and the winds blow over the prairie. Now we have warm shoes to wear under the overshoes. *Wear your shoes with a thankful and a humble heart, for it is not so important what you have on the feet, but it is very important where the feet go.*"

*"It is always possible to be thankful for what is given rather than to complain about what is not given. One or the other becomes a habit of life."*

—ELISABETH ELLIOT, *INSPIRING QUOTATIONS*

Mama was right. As a six-year-old girl I had given my life to Jesus. I knew I belonged to God and that He loved me and had a plan for my life. Then came the choice to obey in small and big things in my everyday living.

My choice now was not "to wear or not to wear" the shoes. Papa had already made that choice!

Mama said I did have a choice in *how* I would wear the shoes—with deep rebellion or with a thankful heart.

Before my beautiful mama went home to be with the Lord, she was asked by my daughter, Janice, "What is the secret to a happy, victorious Christian life?"

"Oh, ja, it is a thankful heart. In everything give thanks—it is the will of God."

God has reminded me from that day to this that we don't have a choice in many events that come our way—the "high button shoes" we don't want—but we *do* have a choice in how we receive them.

*Be cheerful no matter what; pray all the time;*
*thank God no matter what happens.*
*This is the way God wants you*
*who belong to Christ Jesus to live.*
1 Thessalonians 5:16-18, MSG

# String Beans and Credit Cards

CAROL TRAVILLA

LIFE LESSON FROM MOTHER:
*Be resourceful and buy only
what you can pay for.*

*String beans again?* I thought. I didn't say anything—
Mother made us promise we wouldn't complain.

Just six days before this "familiarly green" meal, Mother
had called all seven of us together and announced: "Okay,
everybody, listen up! It's string bean season and I'm getting sick and tired of our mounting bill down at the
grocery store. Mr. Harrison has been very patient to let us
buy our groceries and pay later. But we're getting further
and further behind. I want to pay off that bill.

"If we eat string beans for seven days in a row, I think
we can do it. I'll get a ham bone and a sack of potatoes
to eat with them. I need your support. There will be no
questions like, 'What's for dinner?' And we'll have no
complaints. Okay?"

We nodded in agreement and my brother said, "Let's
go for it."

Each night before we ate our "string bean delight" we
bowed our heads and thanked the Lord for our food. It got
old fast. We missed having meat, salad, and dessert. But we
persevered for Mom. And we accomplished the goal.

I remember how pleased and proud my mother was
the day she walked down the country road to the corner

grocery store and paid off "the bill." Never again were we sent to the store for milk or bread and told to say, "Put it on the bill." We always carried the cash in hand.

*"As soon as you can, pay your debts. As long as you can, give the benefit of the doubt. As much as you can, give thanks. He's already given us more than we deserve."*

—MAX LUCADO, WHEN GOD WHISPERS YOUR NAME

Mother's creative resourcefulness, as well as her determination to meet her goal, made a great impression on me. She made our clothes out of feedbags and she made jam and jelly preserves out of *tomatoes!* For years she acquired our home products through $1 a week catalog sales to her friends.

Mother taught me to face challenges with courage and to be resourceful during the hard times. And today, every time I'm tempted to use a credit card, *I think of string beans!*

*Do you want to be counted wise,*
*to build a reputation for wisdom?*
*Here's what you do:*
*Live well, live wisely, live humbly.*
James 3:13, MSG

# The Homecoming

SHERRIE ELDRIDGE

LIFE LESSON FROM GRANDMA:
*Orphans are the object of God's special
care and protection.*

On the south end of town just across the railroad tracks
was a dilapidated red brick house known as "the county
orphanage." Here many children who had been abandoned
or abused found love. Here they found someone with a
mother's heart big enough to encompass orphans of any
age, race, or background—they found Leah Cook, my
adoptive grandmother.

Leah would be described as a social worker today, but
back in the forties there were no such credentials. She
was simply a dedicated case worker who worked with
county physicians, hospitals, maternity homes, and judges
as an advocate for abandoned children.

On August 4, 1945, Leah received a call from a local
physician, saying that the baby she had been waiting for
had arrived. That baby was me. She and her son and
daughter-in-law had eagerly been anticipating my birth.

My birth mother never saw me. She was counseled to
put her painful past behind her and go on with her life.
Because I was so small at birth, I stayed in an incubator for
eight days and was known by hospital workers as "Baby X."

Leah stood at the nursery window numbed with awe
as she watched the hospital workers prepare me for my
homecoming. They dressed me in a tiny white batiste
dress and a matching bonnet, no bigger than the palm of

a man's hand, then wrapped me in a down-white blanket delicately trimmed with satin ribbons.

"At last you are ours," Leah whispered, as the nurse gently handed me over. I snuggled into her bountiful arms and she carried me through the door.

It was just one block to Retha and Mike's home. Leah's heart pounded as she pulled into the drive. "Here we are, Precious." she said. "This is your home, and now we're going to go in and meet your mommy and daddy."

*"We have a Saviour who has never once failed us. He never will fail us. He has loved and led and guarded us all these years."*

—AMY CARMICHAEL, *YOU ARE MY HIDING PLACE*

Leah pushed the front door open, cradling me in her arms. This moment became the basis of "my adoption story," which my dad recounted with delight until his dying day. "I'll never forget when Mother brought you home from the hospital," he would say. "It seems like yesterday when I saw her come through the front door. You were so tiny that she held you in the palm of her hand."

Grandma Leah was God's special angel. When I was orphaned and abandoned, God sent my grandmother to arrange my adoption. When I had no home, parents, or a name, He gave me all three.

*"I will not leave you orphaned.
I'm coming back."*

John 14:18, MSG

# My Mother's Songs

### Dee Brestin

LIFE LESSON FROM MOTHER:
*Sing to your children with psalms, hymns,
and spiritual songs—and the melody will
etch His truths permanently on their hearts.*

Like children on Christmas Eve, our family waited excitedly, peering out the Des Moines airport window, hoping to catch sight of the jet that would land with our new five-year-old Korean daughter. Other adoptive families stood with us, clutching balloons, teddy bears, and camcorders.

Finally, we heard, "Here it comes!" Mothers bit their nails, fathers adjusted their video cameras, and children pressed their noses and hands against the window. After an endless minute, the door to Gate A-7 opened. One by one an adult who functioned as a "traveling companion" walked through the door with a black-haired baby, called out a name, and was met with tears and hugs from the new parents, siblings, and extended family.

Then, with emotion causing his voice to catch, Steve, my husband, said, *"I see her."* With one hand, Annie reached straight up to cling to the woman's hand, with the other she clutched her only possession—the bag of airplane toys given to her by the flight attendant. She was wearing yellow footed pajamas that had "Seoul Olympics" printed all over them. Her dark eyes were wide with fear.

All we could do with our limited language skills was to hug her, stroke her black silky hair, and give her the stuffed bunny we had bought as a welcoming gift. We did tell her that I was her "ohma" (mother) and that Steve was her "appa" (father). Her black eyes looked blank. How I wanted to assure her that everything was going to be all right — that we were going to love and care for her. I wanted to tell her that the Lord had led us together and that we belonged to a good God who does all things well, so there was no reason to fear. But all that would have to wait. Steve took her little hand in his big one and we walked, as a family, to the car.

The next six months were trying. Annie was withdrawn and unresponsive. She seldom laughed or cried the way normal five-year-olds do, but seemed like a little stone. We lavished her with attention, hoping to coax her, like a frightened turtle, out of her seemingly impenetrable shell. Nothing seemed to be working.

In addition, the attention we lavished on Annie seemed to cause great pain to Sally, our youngest biological child. Our sunshiny eleven-year-old retreated behind clouds of gloom and anxiety. She was having trouble sleeping, was losing weight, and was exhibiting the symptoms of full-blown clinical depression. I was frustrated and sometimes wanted to tell Sally to *snap out of it!* Didn't she realize how much we loved her? My husband, who has the gift of mercy and is more understanding of depression, said, "Just think of Sally as having the flu. You wouldn't tell someone who has the flu to snap out of it!"

I remember one morning during my quiet time that I cried out my frustration: "Lord, I thought You led us to do this! I never would have done it had I known it was going to ruin Sally's life! Is Satan causing us this trouble? Or did we take the wrong road?" Engulfed in self-pity, tears ran down my cheeks. "Lord, please help us!" I cried.

At that moment a song my mother sang over and over again from the Psalms when I was a child came to my mind. I could almost hear her lilting soprano:

The Lord is my light and my salvation.
Whom then shall I fear, whom then shall I fear?
The Lord is the strength of my life,
The Lord is the strength of my life,
Of whom then shall I be afraid?[1]

It was as if the Lord was saying to me. "With my true light I led you down this path. Now, during this time of darkness, trust Me. Trust Me."

And God proved Himself trustworthy indeed. One of the first things that happened after that morning was that my husband Steve said he felt it was time to get Sally medical help. A physician himself, he believed that the stress Sally was experiencing may have revealed a chemical imbalance in her body.[2]

Tests revealed that Sally indeed was experiencing an imbalance. After she had been on medication for a month, we began to see a real change in her. She started sleeping, eating, and laughing again. She still, however, had to deal with her spiritual struggle of jealousy toward her sister.

Sally explains how God brought her through that hurdle as well. "I was feeling good enough to go out again and I went with my family to a Christian concert. Afterwards there was an altar call for salvation and for recommitment. I went forward and knelt before the Lord and said, 'Lord, I know I am supposed to love my new sister—but I don't. You know the yuk and the jealousy that has been in my heart. Oh Lord, I am so sorry—but I need

Your help. I can't seem to do this on my own. Please take away the yuk and fill me with love for Annie.'"

Amazingly, God did exactly that. He bent down and listened to that eleven-year-old's repentant cry and filled her with love for her sister. Sally's new love toward her sister also proved to be the turning point in Annie's life. Annie needed not only her parents' love, but her sister's love. As Sally began to play with her, laugh with her, and love her, Annie began to brighten, like a parched flower who has been given a good drink.

*"I have made a lifetime commitment to bank my life on the Word of God—and God has honored that commitment. And yet, there have been times . . . when my feelings have screamed 180 degrees in the opposite direction of God's Word . . . lots of times."*

—NEY BAILEY, *FAITH IS NOT A FEELING*

My mother did not talk to me about spiritual things the way I do with my children, but she did sing. She sang while she did her housework, while we traveled in the car, when she woke us up, and when she tucked us in. She sang many kinds of songs, but often they were hymns and spiritual songs. It surprised me, when I gave my life to Christ as a young woman, how many Scriptures I already knew—because they had been the lyrics to so many of Mother's songs. I wasn't sure if my mother chose to sing those songs because she believed them or because scriptural songs tend to be so beautiful, written by the greatest Poet of all.

Recently, I had a discussion with my eighty-four-year-old mother that was a great comfort to me. She said, "Do you remember when I would sit down at the piano and sing: 'The Lord is my Light and my Salvation?'"

I said, "Yes, Mother—of course I do."

"When people would be unkind to me, or when life would be hard, I found great comfort in that song. I meant those words, Dee." And then, over the phone, while I wept, she sang them to me again:

> The Lord is my light and my salvation.
> Whom then shall I fear, whom then shall I fear?
> The Lord is the strength of my life,
> The Lord is the strength of my life,
> Of whom then shall I be afraid?

*Speak to one another with psalms,*
*hymns and spiritual songs. Sing and make music*
*in your heart to the Lord, always giving thanks*
*to God the Father for everything, in the name*
*of our Lord Jesus Christ.*
Ephesians 5:19-20

# A Lesson Beyond the Grave

DEE JEPSEN

LIFE LESSON FROM MOTHER:
*What mothers say and the example they set
will speak to their children long after they
are gone.*

God's kindness and mercy never cease to amaze me. It makes me feel very grateful and humble to think that the Creator of the universe gives time and attention to happenings in our everyday lives. Sometimes we are very aware of His interest and guidance. There are also times when we don't realize His involvement and its impact on us until many years later. A conversation I overheard as a thirteen-year-old girl has had an impact on my life for nearly fifty years — until this very day!

My mother, Helen, had died of a brain tumor a few weeks before this particular afternoon when my aunt and grandmother sat together in the parlor of the white house, sharing their grief. I happened to be in the next room and overheard their conversation. Grandma was saying, "Yes, Helen was a good girl. Did you hear about the time she had with her boss when she was a legal secretary downtown?"

My aunt acknowledged that she had not.

"Well," Grandma continued, "when Helen worked for that lawyer downtown, there was a parade one day that went down the street in front of the office. Helen went to the second floor window to look out and her boss came and stood next to her. He was a married man, and when he moved up close to her and put his arm around her waist, Helen went over to her desk, picked up her purse, and said, 'I'm going to have to quit.' *And she did.* That's the kind of girl Helen was."

Today an incident like that would likely result in a charge of sexual harassment. My mother lost a job. Yet in my heart of hearts I know that she would feel it was a small price to pay for God to deliver a message to me about virtue and self-respect.

*"There is no more influential or powerful role on earth than a mother's. Their words are never fully forgotten, their touch leaves an indelible impression, and the memory of their presence lasts a lifetime."*

—CHARLES SWINDOLL, *GROWING WISE IN FAMILY LIFE*

I've never forgotten that story, even though its impact was not clear to me for a number of years. I am convinced that conversation—and the fact that I heard it from the next room—was not just "happenstance." It was a merciful heavenly Father's way of providing a mother's guidance to a young girl who could no longer receive it from her mother in person. It was a lesson I never forgot.

*So let God work his will in you.*
*Yell a loud no to the Devil and watch him scamper.*
*Say a quiet yes to God and he'll be there in no time. . . .*
*Purify your inner life.*
James 4:7-8, MSG

# Sweet Dreams

JEANNETTE CLIFT GEORGE

LIFE LESSON FROM MOTHER:
*Nurture the unique creativity
in every individual.*

My mother was a gifted pianist. Music never left her fingers, her heart, or her home. Even though she gave up a concert career when she married my father, she loved to play the piano and she thought I would feel the same.

I practiced obediently, if not skillfully, doing endless scales or one-note melodies punctuated by chords repeated with little variation. My assigned music was in a large and floppy collection that kept sliding off the piano as though it, too, wanted to leave the room. I was *not* a gifted student. At a piano recital, I took twelve emotion-packed minutes to introduce my piece, which I forgot the moment I sat down to play it.

One afternoon I was laboring joylessly over "The Happy Farmer," and Mother was out in the backyard laboring with *great* joy over her day lilies. As I played, Mother called from the yard, "No, it's F-sharp, honey, F-sharp!"

I struck every note my two hands could reach and began to cry. Mother hurried in to me. "What's the matter?" she asked.

"How did you know it was wrong?" I cried. "You were out in the yard and I was here with the music. What I played sounded just fine to me!"

Mother looked at me in dismay. She had not intended to discourage me. "Besides," I said, still spattering tears upon the keyboard, "I'm only doing this to please you."

My mother stared at me in astonishment. Never in her life had she imagined that anyone did not *want* to play the piano. All her dreams of handing down the joy of music to her daughter melted in the glare of my outburst. And in one instant, she accepted the painful revelation.

She came to me, smiling, and hugged me. She brushed away my tears and said, "Well, honey, you don't have to do it. We'll find something that pleases you."

*"God is for you. Turn to the sidelines;*
*that's God cheering your run.*
*Look past the finish line;*
*that's God applauding your steps.*
*Listen for him in the bleachers,*
*shouting your name. Too tired to continue?*
*He'll carry you. Too discouraged to fight?*
*He's picking you up. God is for you."*

—MAX LUCADO, *IN THE GRIP OF GRACE*

Now I wish I had learned to play the piano, but I think back to that moment in awed awareness of my mother's love for me. A love so personalized that I did not have to live out *her* dream. She freed me to pursue my own dream: theater.

My mother and father attended every performance of mine in the Houston area. No matter how demanding the role or how critical the production, my mother would always say, "Sugar, you can do it. I know you can." And something in me deeper than fear and doubt believed her. Even in the wearying long hours of rehearsals and performances my mother's creative encouragement was a joy.

One night after a late performance that had been further lengthened by a picture call, I came home after Mother had gone to bed. There was a light on in the kitchen and downstairs hallway. Tiptoeing, I climbed the stairs to my room. I was very tired, and in that moment stumbled upon the deep loneliness that seems to haunt the actor after working hours. As I moved to turn off the light, I glanced down the stairwell.

A large chrysanthemum plant was on a table in the hallway. That night it bloomed with greetings from my mother. She had cut out tissue paper faces and placed them in the center of each blossom, and had printed messages on the border of each face . . . "Good Night, Jeannette . . . Sweet Dreams." No bouquet ever meant more to me or has stayed so fresh in my memory. When I think of how God has gifted each of us with our own unique creativity, I think of those flowers, and I thank God for my mother.

*The boundary lines have fallen for me in pleasant places; surely I have a delightful inheritance.*

Psalm 16:6

# The Great Adventure

CYNTHIA FANTASIA

LIFE LESSON FROM MOTHER:
*God is big enough and strong enough to
handle anything you bring to him.*

"But she's so young," my mother said.

Grammy was quick to respond. "Don't you trust me?
Do you want me to go by myself? Why don't *you* come
with me then?"

"How can I? I also have a five-year-old. I can't leave
her for all that time!"

"Well then, let Cynthia come with me. It'll be good for
her. A better education than she would get at school!"

"You mean you want to go during the school year?"

"Of course. It's too hot in the summer. And she'll learn
more there than she would in school. What's six weeks,
anyway? And I can't go alone. Besides, if you say no, I may
never get to see my sister again—and it's been forty-four
years!"

That was it. Grammy had played her trump card. No
daughter would ever stand in the way of an old woman
seeing her sister. I guessed I would be going somewhere
with my grandmother for six weeks—the *when* and the
*where* were still a mystery. I later learned that I was to
travel to Italy with my grandmother to visit relatives and
friends in her hometown.

I was eleven years old, both eager and frightened
about going so far away for so long a time. Was God big
enough to know what was going on? Did He know I was

going to Italy for six weeks with my grandmother? Did He know that the flight would take a total of twenty-four hours? (This was long before jet travel.) Did He know that I was scared and excited—all at the same time? "Is He big enough for *that,* Mom?" I asked.

With a gentle hug and a kiss on my forehead, she whispered, "I wouldn't let you go if I didn't believe that." I know now that perhaps the best gift a mother can give her daughter is to encourage her to go places she has never been before, trusting that our strong God is big enough to meet her there. So off I went on the greatest adventure of my life!

*"I wish for you the joy of holding life
with an open hand. Just let go of all the stuff
you've had to worry about and hang on to
and protect . . . It isn't what you have
that determines your strength now
or in the future. It is what you are
willing to let go of that is
the ultimate test."*

—BOB BENSON, *SEE YOU AT THE HOUSE*

Every day for six weeks at least one letter would arrive for me. That familiar handwriting was my daily assurance of my mother's love. I would read and reread those letters as she rambled on about what they ate, who she talked to, what she did, the weather, the news from home, but most of all how she loved me and was grateful that her little girl had this wonderful opportunity.

In Mother's letters she always reminded me of the greatness and bigness of God. "You know," she would say at the end of every letter, "I stood out on the porch last night and looked up to the sky, at the moon and stars, and I prayed for you: 'Dear God, my little girl is so far away. But You are so great and so big, and You placed those stars in the sky, and You placed the moon in exactly the right place. And I know that my little one is looking at the same moon and stars, so we are connected, Lord, through Your hand. Guide and protect her. Amen.'"

Many years have passed since my great adventure to Italy. My own children are growing up too quickly. I've heard some questions with a familiar ring:

"Mom, can I go to Egypt this summer on a missions trip?"

"Mom, can I go to London to see some friends—over Thanksgiving?"

"Mom, can I go to Spain with my class?"

I often find myself standing on our deck late at night, looking up at the sky and praying: "Dear God, my little one is so far away. But You are so great and so big, and You placed those stars in the sky and You hung the moon in exactly the right place. And I know that my child—*Your* child—is looking at the same moon and stars, so we are connected through Your hand. Guide and protect. Amen."

*The God who made the world and everything in it*
*is the Lord of heaven and earth . . . and he determined*
*the times set for them and the exact places*
*where they should live.*
Acts 17:24,26

# Mama's Spring

SANDRA PICKLESIMER ALDRICH

LIFE LESSON FROM MOTHER:
*If we have faith, God will provide.*

In the summer of 1944, when my mother was barely pregnant with me, and my father was away in the army, the wells in our area of Harlan County, Kentucky, went dry. The drought was so bad that even the nearby Cumberland River was dangerously low.

My grandparents and my mother carried river water up a steep bank to wash clothes in, but first the water had to be poured through several layers of thin cloth in a futile attempt to strain it.

They also carried water for the flowers that my grandfather's mother, Grandmaw, grew in a narrow strip of soil between the river and the road. The flowers were the one pleasure Grandmaw allowed herself, and she justified their existence by occasionally offering bouquets for sale to travelers.

The drought had taken all but the strongest plants, and these were kept alive by the scant dipperfuls of dirty river water that Grandmaw poured over them, grumbling all the while.

"Mama," as we called my grandmother, would gently remind my great-grandmother that the Lord would send water in His time. Grandmaw usually answered such statements from her daughter-in-law with silence. But one afternoon, she gave an exasperated snort.

"You tellin' me that feller's interested in gettin' us

water? I wouldn't count on that if I was you."

Mama wasn't one to let her faith be challenged without an answer. "Now, Grandma, I don't know how He's gonna help us, but He will. Maybe it'll be as simple as keeping us strong enough to lug the water up the river bank. Or maybe, when He's through teaching us more about faith and patience, He'll give us a good rain shower."

Grandmaw searched the cloudless blue sky above the mountains and snorted again. "Why don't you just ask for a spring of water? You're just as likely to get the one as the other." Then she turned and went back into the house.

Our brick home was well built, but it had revealed one flaw in the heavy rains that fell shortly after its construction a decade before. A leak had appeared in the corner of the basement. My grandfather, who had built the house with his sons, had dug a three-foot-deep basin to contain the water. Then the leak disappeared just as strangely as it had appeared, and the basin remained dry for those ten years.

After one particularly tiring day of lugging water for the wash, Mama stretched out on the sofa in the living room, her very sighs a prayer for water. Almost immediately, she was off the sofa and calling for my mother.

"Wilma, come with me! The Lord just showed me the prettiest stream of water flowing from under my head. He's got water for us!"

Before my mother could catch up to her, Mama had grabbed a chisel and headed for the basement. Without hesitation, she broke through the thin concrete of the basin and began to chop through the clay underneath.

"The sofa is right over this spot. I know the water's right here."

When several minutes of enthusiastic digging produced nothing, Mama prayed aloud, "Now, Lord, You showed me the water. Help me hit it this time."

Suddenly, the clay grew dark around the chisel, and soon water bubbled up over the spot. Mama quickly stepped out of the basin to keep her feet from getting wet. And all the while she repeatedly said, "Thank you, Lord," as she grabbed my mother and joyously hugged her.

*"Faith is putting all your eggs in
God's basket, then counting your blessings
before they hatch."*

—RAMONA C. CARROLL, *INSPIRING QUOTATIONS*

Grandmaw heard the commotion and came grumbling down the steps. When she saw the basin filling with fresh, clean water, she was speechless for a moment.

Mama called her to come closer. "Look, Grandmaw! The Lord gave us water. And there'll be plenty for your flowers. You'll never have to pour river water over them ever again!"

By then Grandmaw had found her voice. "What are you sayin'? You think just because there's a bit of water there today that it's gonna be there forever? That'll be all seeped out by mornin'."

Mama never stopped smiling. "Oh, no, it won't! The Lord gave it, and He won't let it run out for as long as this family needs it. And to think it was here all the time, just waiting for us. Oh, He's so good. If we only have faith, He always provides."

She was right. Grandmaw never had to use river water again for her flowers. Not only did the spring supply water for us, but there was enough for all of the neighbors in our little community, too. Mama refused to be stingy with what the Lord had given. And the spring never went dry as long as a member of our extended family owned the house.

When I last saw the basin in the late 1960s—just before the house was sold—it was still full of clear spring water. Oh, I know there are those who would say that Mama's subconscious mind knew that the water was there because of the leak ten years before, but she wouldn't have accepted such reasoning.

Still, I can hear her retelling the story and adding, "And to think He even provided the basin before we needed it."

I often think about that family story and wonder how many things He has provided for me, but I've not claimed them. How many springs within my own life—just as precious as Mama's—are just waiting to be released by faith?

> *"The simple truth is that if you had*
> *a mere kernel of faith, a poppy seed, say,*
> *you would tell this mountain, 'Move!'*
> *and it would move. There is nothing*
> *you wouldn't be able to tackle."*
> Matthew 17:20, MSG

# When Life Isn't Fair

Dr. Karen Johnson Hayter

LIFE LESSON FROM MOTHER:
*You will never be alone.*

Every day for months after the marital separation, I felt like I was sludging through quicksand, grabbing at every branch—or at every person—yelling, "Help me! I can't stand this pain." I woke up at 3:30 A.M. every morning, feeling like I had been kicked in the stomach as I remembered that my marriage of twenty-seven years was over. While I attempted to do a daily live television program, weeping almost every hour, I truthfully felt my life was over, and often thought dying would have been preferable.

One source of light during this dark period was my mother. A widow, and seventy-eight years old, mother held me and cried with me, and then she mobilized her forces. She enlisted family and friends to get me moved into an apartment. She encouraged me to "just keep breathing," and she provided incredible moral support. I was covered with her prayers. Mother's heart was breaking, too, but she attempted to bring positive reinforcement to my life every day—without being a Pollyanna.

Mom called almost daily to tell me an uplifting story or amusing anecdote, even though I didn't laugh most of the time. She firmly encouraged me by saying, "Get up, get going, keep moving! God has not forgotten you!" And sometimes she just held the phone as I cried and spoke of my hurt.

"Karen, God will never leave you," she said repeatedly. "Hold on to the things God has told you in the light.

They are still true in the darkest times."

I slowly uncovered my most terrifying and paralyzing fear—*being alone for the rest of my life.* I am an only child. My husband and I were unable to have children. I had always envisioned that we would grow old together, travel, enjoy our friends, and continue to minister together for God. It never occurred to me how tightly I held that fantasy until my husband told me he wanted a divorce.

*"We need to let God be God, hour by hour, day by day, experience by experience, time after time . . . And we lie there, praying that the Lord won't let us waste what is going on in any way: 'Help me, Lord, to be what You want me to be in this, to learn what You want me to learn in this, to demonstrate what You want me to demonstrate in this . . . '"*

—EDITH SCHAEFFER, *AFFLICTION*

I felt I had been thrown out to utter darkness—that I would be totally alone forever. When I finally brought that fear into the dimmest of light, it was Mom who reminded me of Hebrews 13:5: "Never will I leave you; never will I forsake you."

"Karen," she would say, "you may be lonely, and you may be in that apartment by yourself, but you are never alone. God will always be there, and He will always be to you whatever you need the most." What I thought I needed

most was a husband—*and the one I had did not want me.*
The rejection I felt was tangible—from him, from some of
my friends, and even from my church.

One day a friend in media ministry gave me a verse of
Scripture. "For Your Maker is your husband . . ." (Isaiah
54:5). What I wanted was a husband with skin on, but that
verse intrigued me. Could it be true? Could God—*the God
of the universe*—be my husband? Could He do the many
things a husband is supposed to do—love me, cherish
me, care for me? Why would He *want* to do that?

Mom's voice came back to me. "Because He *does* love
you with such a great love that it is difficult to comprehend."
Continually, she sent me back to God's Word and to His
promises.

Those great life-giving promises came back to me in
God-initiated, unexpected ways. A friend sent flowers.
People called to say God had put me on their hearts. I
would receive a spontaneous hug during a difficult day.
Over and over, in unanticipated, surprising ways, God was
faithful to his promises.

Healing is slow. I often scrape the scab off an almost-
healed sore. But I am able to continue on and hope for
better days because of God's provision, because of support
from friends, and because of Mom's consistent reminder:
"You will *never* be alone. God will *always* be with you."

*When my soul is in the dumps,*
*I rehearse everything I know of You . . .*
*Fix my eyes on God—*
*soon I'll be praising again.*
*He puts a smile on my face.*
*He's my God.*
Psalm 42:6,11, MSG

# The Harmonica Lady

DAISY HEPBURN

LIFE LESSON FROM MOTHER-IN-LAW:
*God has gifted each of us with the ability
to fulfill His will individually, in separate
styles, but as character copies of
the Lord Jesus.*

Rose Hepburn was the wife of the divisional commander of the Salvation Army in Philadelphia. At the outset of World War II, when veterans began arriving at the newly established Valley Forge Hospital in Pennsylvania, Mother Hepburn began a program of visitation and encouragement to these veterans, most of whom were blind. Along with Mother, a group of Salvationists went every Monday evening for twenty-six years, without fail, until that hospital closed its doors.

On one of the visits Mother met a young man who had requested a harmonica. This was not unusual. Mother was teaching people how to restring violins and work with other musical instruments. Today it might be called "therapy," but then it was just Mother Hepburn's way of making the men feel confident and useful.

Mother loved a challenge. She didn't know where to come up with harmonicas, but she was determined to do so, and God would provide. God answered her prayer by giving her an idea. Somehow, in her own unique way, Mother got in touch with Kate Smith, a well-known singer, and asked if she could help.

On a radio station in Philadelphia, where Mother

Hepburn hosted a broadcast called "The Home League of the Air," she made an appeal for harmonicas for the blinded veterans. With Kate Smith's celebrity status, and the forum of the air waves, the appeal was a success.

My husband says that as a young man, he was simply astounded. "I never saw anything like it. There were thousands of harmonicas. And so many different kinds! The response was so overwhelming that I wouldn't be surprised if everyone in Valley Forge had a harmonica in every pocket!"

*"Whatever God gives you to do,*
*do it as well as you can. This is the best*
*possible preparation for what He*
*may want you to do next."*

—GEORGE MACDONALD,
*GREAT QUOTES & ILLUSTRATIONS*

Over the years Mother established correspondence with those blinded veterans. Many recuperated and were sent to their home towns. When Mother would travel with Dad Hepburn in his ministry, she would often phone or even visit veterans in their homes.

When Mother went to heaven in 1974, we found an up-to-date cross-reference file of over five thousand blinded veterans she kept in touch with through at least a yearly Christmas letter. Besides that, she managed to maintain a regular column in the *Blinded Veterans Newspaper* entitled, "Mrs. Hepburn Chats . . ." She always laughed about the time when, as a guest speaker, someone introduced her in all seriousness as "Mrs. Chats."

It wasn't surprising that Mother became Woman of the Year for the Veteran's Association in Washington. But her honors reflected treasures in heaven.

Only eternity will reveal the lives she influenced and encouraged through this rare ministry, which was certainly an adjunct to her full vocation as national director of women's ministries for the Salvation Army.[1]

*God's various gifts are handed out everywhere;*
*but they all originate in God's Spirit. . . .*
*God's various expressions of power*
*are in action everywhere;*
*but God Himself is behind it all.*
*Each person is given something to do*
*that shows who God is. . . .*
1 Corinthians 12:4-7, MSG

*Go after a life of love as if your life depended on it—*
*because it does. Give yourselves to the gifts God gives*
*you. Most of all, try to proclaim His truth.*
1 Corinthians 14:1, MSG

# Invisible Gold

MARY FARRAR

LIFE LESSON FROM MOTHER:
*Mothers have incredible power
to nurture their child's inner strength.
Such "gold" lasts a lifetime.*

My mother once taught me the secret of success—an invaluable lesson I have never forgotten. In fact, I used it as recently as last week, on the night our son played his first high school football game. Let me explain.

In Texas, we take our football seriously. I mean, it's right up there with God. In our little town, the football players are demi-gods and the cheerleaders are the archangels. Every Friday night the faithful gather in our brilliantly lit new AstroTurf cathedral. (Our school library stinks, but it can wait.) And what a service it is, as we worship in one accord! Bands blare, drill teams kick, flag girls float, cheerleaders flip-flop . . . and parents lose all sense of inhibition.

The diehards paint their faces and wave cowbells, while the rest of us don brilliant hats and garish earrings, and only moderately embarrass our children. The entire lot of us whoop and holler, yelling barbaric brutalities like, "Whomp 'em up side of the head!", "Crush them!!", "KILL THEM!!!", "SMASH THEM INTO THE GROUND!!!" Anywhere else, such verbal assault would be grounds for arrest. But here, all is understood. We have been rendered temporarily insane by the Great Football Spirit.

You may think I'm kidding, but any state in which a cheerleader mom hires a hit man to kill another cheerleader's mom is a state that definitely takes its football seriously.

And now my oldest son is playing football in Texas. Needless to say, the pressure to succeed is fairly intense.

The night before his first game, he could barely sleep a wink. He kept feeling the hot breath of his opponent, the rush of adrenaline as helmets clashed, the grinding impact of bodies colliding. The anticipation was almost too much.

And then game night arrived. He put on his knee pads, thigh pads, shoulder pads, waist pads, cleats, helmet, arm protectors, chin protector, and mouthpiece. (I admit to you, for one brief moment I had second thoughts. But, alas, it was too late.) If we hadn't known he was Number Eighty, we never would have recognized him. And so we were off.

From the first kickoff of the game, we cheered. We cheered for the receiver, the quarterback, the linebackers, the water boy, *anybody* who had on a red-and-black jersey. But for three straight quarters, John just stood on the sidelines. He didn't play one single down. As the minutes ticked by, we were beginning to wonder if Number Eighty would ever get his moment of glory.

And then the coach motioned. John grabbed his helmet and ran into the backfield. The first play, the quarterback took the ball and was tackled instantaneously. The play was over before anyone could even blink an eyelid. As the team lined up for the next play, I could see John shaking his hands with determination. He was determined to be part of the action, even if it killed him. The ball was snapped and John flew into action.

"What a great block!" my husband, Steve, shouted. "He nailed the guy!!"

When the air had finally cleared, we searched for John,

but he wasn't on the field. He had been pulled out of the game and put back on the sidelines.

Two plays. He had only been part of two measly plays! Moments later the game was over, and everyone started to head for home. I had a sick feeling in my stomach . . . a sad sense of incompletion.

As I pulled up to the locker rooms and saw the dejected figure huddled over his helmet, I knew that John felt far worse than I did.

"Mom, I don't want to talk about it," he said, getting into the car. "I was terrible. I blew it. This was my big chance, and I blew it."

"What do you mean, you blew it?" I wasn't prepared for this. I am not a football genius, but I could hardly imagine that two plays consisted of total failure. He had blocked the guy, hadn't he?

"I blocked the wrong guy, Mom! The coach yelled at me and pulled me out of the game. I just blew it, that's all. He'll never put me in again." John was holding back the tears. "Please . . . just take me home. I don't want to see anybody. I am so embarrassed and humiliated."

At that moment, my sanguine son was truly convinced that his football career was over. As we drove home in silence, I prayed for wisdom. I knew my son would recover. Later his dad would point out that at least he had blocked *someone,* and that in due time he would get his blocks straight! But tonight he was hurting, and I needed some of those "apples of gold in settings of silver."

And then I remembered something that had happened years ago. It was the spring of 1973, and I was fresh out of college. My parents were traveling around the world for a month and had left me in charge of my three youngest siblings, ages twelve, fourteen, and sixteen. What I thought would be a simple housekeeper role of cooking, cleaning, making lunches, and washing clothes turned into a crash course in mothering.

Meeting the *emotional* needs of three teenagers was a far greater task than I had ever anticipated.

Each day brought a new crisis. It seemed like I was on the phone to the doctor or the school at least once a week. By the end of the month, I was a nervous wreck. And so were they.

*"The home is the natural habitat*
*for growing human beings*
*and shaping eternal souls."*

—GLORIA GAITHER, *LET'S MAKE A MEMORY*

Just before my parents were due home, my youngest sister, Joy, tried out for cheerleading. It was her first effort at making the big time, and she had no intention of losing due to lack of practice. Our living room became a gymnasium for Joy and her friends, driving us all crazy with their endless cheers and cartwheels and toe-touches. I made an attempt at coaching. By the day of tryouts, I was more nervous than she was. Now all I could do was wait and pray. It was pure torture.

That afternoon when Joy walked in the door, I knew she had lost. I reached for the right words, but they weren't there. And so I blubbered something like, "Oh, Joy, I'm so sorry. You really did deserve it!" and, "Maybe next

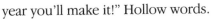

year you'll make it!" Hollow words.

A few days later, much to everyone's relief, my parents returned home. One of the first questions out of Mom's mouth was, "Joy, how did tryouts go?"

We all smothered a gasp.

"I lost," she said, quietly.

"Really?" Mom said easily. There was not an iota of fluster in her voice.

Then, putting her arms around her, she said, "Well, Joy, I am so proud of you for working so very hard, and then for having the courage to go out there and try!"

Joy beamed. Courage. She had demonstrated courage. And she had worked wonderfully hard. Mom may not have realized it, but she had just taken an invisible gold medal and placed it around her daughter's neck. Joy was a winner when it came to *character*.

All my life Mom had emphasized character over accolades. She had reminded me that my hope was in Christ, who looked upon my heart. If He was pleased with me, I had pleased the Greatest One of all! When I succeeded and got a big head, she would gently lower me a few notches. She reminded me that it was God who gave me those abilities, and that it is He who raises one up and puts another down.

On a daily basis Mom had refocused my eyes and placed invisible gold medals around my neck. A medal for kindness here, a medal for personal discipline there. Medals that eventually meant more to me than the praises of a thousand fans.

So there you have it. My mom's secret to success. You can always be a winner when you succeed at character — when you succeed at patience, endurance, faithfulness, kindness, compassion, sacrifice, loyalty, honesty, integrity.

These are the skills that bring true success and the blessing of God in life, in marriage, in parenting, in work. In fact, God promises *more* than success and blessing in this life. He promises a *legacy* of blessing—all the way to our children's children.

And so my mom has passed on the blessing of God to her grandchild, John. That night, after John had gone to bed, this nearly six-foot hunk of a kid called me into his room. The immensity of his despair had subsided by now, and he had begun to realize that life was not over. There would be other football games.

"Mom, next game I'll do you proud, I promise," he said.

"John," I said, "you have already done me proud. You are a man of integrity and character, and there is nothing—and I mean *nothing*—you could do to make me more proud. You could carry the ball for a hundred touchdowns and lead the team to a state victory, and it wouldn't make me any prouder."

"Really?" he said, taking in a huge breath and smiling.

"Really." I replied.

Even in Texas.

*But the lovingkindness of Yahweh*
*is from everlasting to everlasting*
*on those who fear Him, and His faithfulness to do*
*what He has promised is to their children's children,*
*to those who keep His covenant,*
*and who remember His precepts to do them.*
Psalm 103:17-18, NASB

# $\mathcal{A}$ Gentle Rebuke

KATHY COLLARD MILLER

LIFE LESSON FROM MOTHER:
*Every life is valuable.*

As a cocky teen, I thought I knew all about life and truth. One summer, as part of a teen religious organization, I joined my friends on a camping outing. We were having a great time. I was part of the leadership team and thought I had *arrived.* My mother helped to chaperone the event, and we were all sitting together after dinner, talking, when the rumor rippled through the group.

*"God tells man who he is.*
*God tells us that*
*He created man in* His *image.*
*So man is something wonderful."*

—FRANCIS SCHAEFFER, *ESCAPE FROM REASON*

"Did you hear the news? Marilyn Monroe is dead," one girl whispered.

"No!" another girl gasped. "How do you know?"

"Linda says she heard it on the radio. How awful!"

Another girl said, "They say it could be suicide."

I immediately thought, *She didn't have a good*

*reputation anyway,* and without thinking, I blurted, "Oh, well, good riddance!"

Some girls nodded in agreement, but my mother frowned and gently replied, "But Kathy, *every* life is valuable."

I've never forgotten her compassionate rebuke. Whenever I start to think that someone isn't important, I remember my mother's words. Then I'm reminded that in God's eyes, no one is excluded in the truth of John 3:16.

*This is how much God loved the world:*
*He gave His Son, His one and only Son. And this is why:*
*so that no one need be destroyed;*
*by believing in Him,*
*anyone can have a whole and lasting life.*
John 3:16, MSG

# The Welcome Song

JAN CARLBERG

LIFE LESSON FROM MOTHER:
*Jesus won't let you limit the welcome song
to your few favorite verses.*

As a child in Chicago, I remember singing a little song in Sunday school—"There's a welcome here. There's a welcome here. There's a Christian welcome here." We belted it out on cue from our teacher whenever somebody new came to class. I don't know how it really made anybody feel, since it never got sung to me. My daddy was the preacher, so we were supposed to feel welcomed already.

When I was ten years old, Daddy, a Baptist minister, heard the whisper of God and moved us from Illinois to Georgia. They didn't sing the welcome song there—to me or anyone else. It's not that they weren't glad we were there. They just didn't know the song. They needed somebody to teach them. That was Daddy's job. Through sermons and rolled-up sleeves, Mama and Daddy taught and lived the welcome song.

"General welcomes are easy to say or sing," Mama would say, while we worked side by side in her tiny kitchen. Most folks would have had legitimate reasons for not welcoming any newcomers to such cramped quarters. But someone stitched a sampler to underscore Mama's philosophy. It read: SMALL HOUSES FILLED WITH LOVE HAVE ELASTIC WALLS.

Mama and her walls knew how to stretch. And Mama knew how to teach while I reached to peel another potato.

"The welcome song's easy to sing when you're singing to your own kind, Janice. But Jesus had something bigger and better in mind. He wants us to learn a few more verses."

The older I got, the more "verses" Mama and Jesus made me learn. When I was little I sang, "Jesus loves the little children, all the children of the world," but the only black baby I knew, even in Chicago, was the black baby doll my parents gave me. So I practiced loving "all the children of the world" on one black doll. It took many more years to know some red or yellow or black children by name.

*"Jesus has a family in an interracial neighborhood called heaven."*

—AUTHOR UNKNOWN, *DECISION*

*"To be glad instruments of God's love in this imperfect world is the service to which man is called."*

—ALBERT SCHWEITZER, *GREAT QUOTES & ILLUSTRATIONS*

When we moved to the South in the 1950s, we didn't know how threatening the welcome song could be, but Mama refused to stop singing it. Her message was consistent: "Welcomes come in *all* colors, Janice."

My color was accepted—sort of a basic whitish-pink and slightly freckled, but I talked funny. I spoke "Yankee" and they talked "Southern." So I suppose if they'd known "The Welcome Song," they'd have sung me a qualified version. My friends and neighbors came in varying shades of freckled, white, or olive skin, except in summer, when we worked at tanning our hides toward the color that would have been most unwelcome by too many.

A few years and a few lessons later I learned that *people,* not *locations,* had their own way of choosing which people to exclude from the Christian welcome song.

"That's the heart of the problem," Mama would say, "singing the Christian part of the welcome. Jesus won't let you limit the song to your few favorite verses."

Peter, one of the twelve disciples hand-picked by Jesus, knew the song. At least the *general* welcome part most of us are comfortable singing. He was going great until God showed up and taught him the Christian welcome verse through a vision. (Daddy and Mama taught me about it from the Bible, so God didn't have to use such drastic measures on me.) Peter was hungry, not for words, but for regular food. He'd been praying for a long time and while he waited for his host to prepare the food, he fell asleep.

Maybe God said something like, "Peter, let me teach you another verse to your welcome song." Then God taught Peter that what God has made kosher stays kosher. And Peter learned that the Christian welcome verse was not just for Jews, but for *everyone.* The good news of Jesus, the forgiveness of sins, the gifts of the Holy Spirit are for everyone. Then Peter sang his heart out, or more accurately, sang out the heart of his God.

I don't know if they still teach that welcome song in Sunday school, but Mama's still teaching it around her table and through her letters and stories. Her kitchen (with five welcome signs on one wall) says a lot about her. But the way she lives the Christian part of the welcome song speaks wondrously of her God, who loves to show up and teach us to sing another verse!

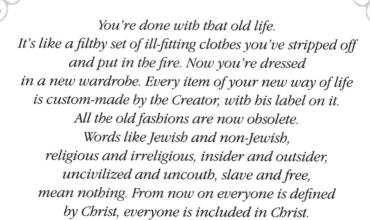

*You're done with that old life.*
*It's like a filthy set of ill-fitting clothes you've stripped off*
*and put in the fire. Now you're dressed*
*in a new wardrobe. Every item of your new way of life*
*is custom-made by the Creator, with his label on it.*
*All the old fashions are now obsolete.*
*Words like Jewish and non-Jewish,*
*religious and irreligious, insider and outsider,*
*uncivilized and uncouth, slave and free,*
*mean nothing. From now on everyone is defined*
*by Christ, everyone is included in Christ.*

Colossians 3:9-11, MSG

# A True Pioneer

NELL MAXWELL

LIFE LESSON FROM MOTHER:
*Do your work with passion and intensity.*

My mother, at age ninety-six, is a true pioneer, and she has left me a lasting legacy. Her mother died in childbirth, so she was raised by her sisters in a little village in the country of Lebanon. Unable to attend school as a child, she is illiterate.

In the early 1900s, faithful missionaries taught my mother the Bible stories she still reflects on today. Even as a child, her keen mind internalized and applied the truth of God's Word—truths she passed on to me. She has always had an indomitable spirit of survival and trust in God.

*"The shocking message of the Bible continues to be that God has chosen the least suspecting of all vessels to do his greatest work. What you are at this particular moment in your life is irrelevant—your nationality, your education, your personality . . . What counts most is* what *and* who *you are willing to become."*

—TIM HANSEL, *HOLY SWEAT*

As I grew up and pursued an education in nursing and then began working with women in Christian ministry, she frequently scolded me for being so involved outside the home. Her cultural background dictated that a woman's place was definitely *in the home*.

As time passed, I caught glimpses of pride in her eyes as she observed what God was doing in the ministry of Women Alive. I especially remember what happened in 1975 at the University of Waterloo at our national convention. There were 4,200 women in the audience and Corrie ten Boom was the speaker. A friend had brought my mother several hundred miles to attend.

I caught sight of Mom entering the auditorium and I left the platform to meet her. The sight of those thousands of women must have been startling and overwhelming to her. Suddenly, placing her arm in mine, she took a long look at the women seated everywhere. Smiling, and with a twinkle in her eye, she spoke up with her Middle Eastern accent and announced, "Look what *we* have done!" I knew she really meant "Look what *God* has done." But in that moment, she and I were one, and the influence and pioneer spirit of her life was articulated in that simple phrase.

*"When God's hand is on you, you run much quicker than you are able."*

—CORRIE TEN BOOM, *CLIPPINGS FROM MY NOTEBOOK*

I jokingly, yet seriously, tell my friends that "I've learned more about living out life's principles at my mother's knee than at any other joint." I've found that the influence of our mothers does not lie in the material possessions they leave us or in whether or not they have had an opportunity for education. It lies in *knowing* God and *knowing who we are in Him.* Once that is settled, we can do the unique work He has for each of us to do with gusto and enthusiasm.

*God smashes the pretensions of the arrogant;*
*he stands with those who have no standing. . . .*
*Fear-of-God is a school in skilled living—*
*first you learn humility, then you experience glory.*
Proverbs 15:25,33; MSG

# Louder Than Words

Julie Baker

LIFE LESSON FROM MOTHER:
*Love is not a feeling; it's an action.*

I hopped out of my best friend's car, closed the door, did a precision-cut pirouette, and pressed my nose against the car window to make a funny face. Finally! This was the last day of my junior year, and I had visions of a summer that included lying out in the sun, reading, and just "hanging out" with my friends.

After skipping up the walkway, I bounded into the house. "Mom! Guess what! I think I aced my English final!" I raced into the family room where my mom was sitting in the gold wing-back chair. She greeted me with a strained smile. Her eyes were streaked with cried-off mascara.

"Mom, what's wrong?"

"Well, you know how your dad always says that it's not sold until they've signed on the dotted line? The sale of one of the spec houses fell through today."

I shrugged and said, "It'll be okay, Mom. It will sell to someone else. What's for dinner?"

I had grown up around the construction business and had some inkling as to the pressures involved, but we'd never really faced a tough time before, so why worry about it? Anyway, I was a *Senior* now!

That was the only time Mom and I discussed the impending economic doom. A "For Sale" sign quickly appeared in our yard. An occupied home usually sells before a new home that lacks curtains and furnishings.

That meant we would be moving. Again.

A few weeks passed and I could hear my parents quietly discussing the skyrocketing interest rates. I knew the housing market was in trouble. Every month they had to pay the mortgage on the house we lived in *and* on the other three houses dad was building. I finally realized the seriousness of the situation.

The "Life of Riley" summer I had dreamed of turned into a demonstration of the Puritan work ethic. The three unsold houses needed landscaping. To save money, my father loaded up his lawn tractor and other equipment and headed over to the first yard.

Side by side, he and Mom picked up large rocks and clumps out of the yards and threw them into the trailer. They took turns driving the tractor and dragging the lawn to level out the rough spots. Then they got out the hand rakes and began the back-breaking task of raking out the small stones.

Not wanting to miss out on the "fun," I joined in. I can still see Dad sitting on that tractor, wearing his old blue fishing hat that he'd never fished in, a white T-shirt, and a pair of blue jeans. Right behind him was Mom in a sleeveless tank top and shorts. We were covered with dust, and sweat trickled down our filthy faces and necks, making dark streaks on our skin.

Mother dug holes for shrubbery and then carried heavy pails of water to irrigate the newly planted bushes. In spite of the work gloves, her hands became blistered.

When the yard was seeded, she planned her days around the watering schedule so she could switch sprinklers. She and Dad repeated the lawn routine until each of the empty, unsold houses had seeded lawns and shrubs.

In the evenings, Mom retreated to the home office. I

could hear the click, click of the adding machine. She was keeping the books for the building business. Somehow the laundry got done and meals were prepared. And she was always at the piano on Sunday morning to play for the worship services.

Then one day our house sold. I wondered which of the new, unsold houses we would move into. It had become a regular routine for us just about every two years. Since we usually stayed in the same school system, I never complained about living in another new house.

*"I am not afraid of storms,*
*for I am learning how to sail my ship."*

—LOUISA MAY ALCOTT, QUOTED IN *LESSONS FROM MOM*

But this time was different. This year the house behind our inner-city church became our residence. The neighborhood thrived on drug deals, shootings, and thefts. The house was filthy and smelled of mildew and fuel oil. The bathtub was crusted with accumulated grime.

Most of our belongings stayed in boxes that we stored in a spare bedroom. At night I could hear mice scampering around and scratching at the boxes. And I prayed those houses would sell soon.

When classes started in the fall, Mom drove me to school and picked me up every day. I later found out that after she dropped me off, she went to a private daycare center and worked for minimum wages to bring in some extra cash. I never heard her complain. And I never saw her cry again.

The houses eventually sold—but not before causing a severe cash flow crisis for Dad's business. And we lived in that dilapidated house until I left for college.

I landed a job as an executive secretary for the summer and added that income to the baby-sitting money I had saved since I was thirteen. It was just enough to attend one year of college. Before leaving, I spent a few quiet moments with my mother. I asked her how she dealt with the disappointment of such devastating financial setbacks.

"I remember when your daddy's mom and dad went through a very difficult time," she said. "Remember the service station Papa owned? Well, one day the city came in and shut off the main street that accessed the station so the roads could be paved with bricks. It cut off most of the traffic to the station for months, and the business dried up.

"Grandma didn't waste time. She approached everyone she could think of who could afford laundry service, and she took in washing and ironing. She worked day and night with just a wringer washer so they could have a little bit of money to live on until the service station business could resume.

"I also remember a time during the war when Papa couldn't find young men to pump the gas and service the customers. Grandma would bundle up and wait on the customers. I never heard her complain. And I never saw her cry."

Mom's words would come back to encourage me when my own husband lost his lucrative mid-management position with an oil company. For the next four years I watched my well-educated and well-connected husband struggle to find full-time employment. I thought about my mother as I took a temporary job pulling out staples for eight hours a day to bring in extra cash. Then came an insurance job I detested. Once again the memories of my mother and my grandmother kept me from complaining.

Our daughter spent her entire high school experience— not just her senior year—watching her family's material possessions being used up and taken away. She's a college student now. Recently I found this note in my mailbox:

*Dear Mom,*

*Being on my own this year has taught me how difficult it can be to manage my own finances.... It's frustrating to find that many of the girls on my floor have access to their parents' credit cards and cash without the responsibility of having a job.*

*I've thought back on the last four years as you and Dad were struggling to support us and want you to know that I'm beginning to understand the hardship you experienced...*

*I saw you come alongside Dad and be his partner. I saw the sacrifices you both made so that Steve and I could have food and clothing. I saw how you never stopped singing in church or volunteering your time when things were tough. I saw how you continued to read your Bible, write new songs, and tell others about Jesus, even in the midst of financial ruin....*

*I know that you may not have earthly riches to leave behind to us kids, but I have already received my inheritance.... You've taught me that God is in control no matter what situation we face....*

*I thank you and Dad for your commitment to each other and to the Lord.... You may look at those years as years of loss, but I look at them as years of gain.... You've taught me that love is not a feeling, but an action.*

*Love,*

*Christy*

*So we're not giving up. How could we!
Even though on the outside it often looks like things
are falling apart on us, on the inside, where God is
making new life, not a day goes by without his
unfolding grace. These hard times are small potatoes
compared to the coming good times, the lavish
celebration prepared for us. . . . The things we see now
are here today, gone tomorrow.
But the things we can't see now will last forever.*
2 Corinthians 4:16-18, MSG

# Playing with Fire

BARBI FRANKLIN

LIFE LESSON FROM MOTHER:
*Discipline is never enjoyable,*
*but it is essential to spiritual maturity.*

It happened in "the pink room." I don't remember which
one of us came up with the idea first, but my sisters and
I whispered and giggled all the way up the stairs as we
carried matchbooks.

Quietly and carefully we pulled the trundle bed out
from under the triple bunk bed and slid into the open
space under the bunks. Looking at each other with mis-
chief in our eyes, we embarked on our adventure.

*"Parents who hope to shape their children's*
*wills with wisdom need to blend a lot of*
*love and affirmation into their discipline."*

—CHARLES SWINDOLL, *GROWING WISE IN FAMILY LIFE*

One by one we took turns lighting matches and
blowing them out. We lingered over each one. The
flames flickered with different colors as we blew on the
fire produced by each match. Smothering our giggles,
we watched the smoke rise from the burned matches

after we blew out the flames and dutifully placed the used matches in a pile on the pink carpet.

After a while we were having so much fun we didn't even take turns. We just kept lighting the matches and blowing them out. Our little pile had grown substantially and we never noticed the smoke that was rising from the center of the pile.

Our party abruptly ended the moment we heard our mother on the stairs. Panic struck. She smelled smoke and was shocked to find three of her four precious little girls millimeters away from starting a fire that could have burned down the house and taken their lives!

We had been warned about playing with matches, so we knew we were in trouble. One at a time Mom talked to us about what we had done to disobey her. She longed to show us mercy and yet still get the point across. After each "talk," she quietly said, "If you are willing to be disciplined, lay over my knee and the spanking will be much easier. But if I have to force you over my knee, it will be much harder." One by one we reluctantly, though voluntarily, lay over her knee and took the consequences for our disobedience.

*"Every great person has first learned* how *to* *obey,* whom *to obey, and* when *to obey."*

—WILLIAM WARD, *QUOTABLE QUOTATIONS*

This incident left a profound impression on my four-year-old mind. I began to understand God's character in a new way. Today I find myself in a society that frowns on any kind of physical discipline. On many days I struggle over the balance between discipline and mercy. However, the day I played with fire reminds me that God used my mother's loving but firm hand to teach me a lesson for a lifetime. *Discipline is never enjoyable, but it is essential to spiritual maturity.*

*Give yourselves to disciplined instruction;*
*open your ears to tested knowledge.*
*Don't be afraid to correct your young ones;*
*a spanking won't kill them. A good spanking, in fact,*
*might save them from something worse than death.*
*Dear child, if you become wise, I'll be one happy*
*parent. My heart will dance and sing*
*to the tuneful truth you'll speak.*

Proverbs 23:12-16, MSG

# A Cruel Remark

CAROL KENT

LIFE LESSON FROM MOTHER-IN-LAW:
*Don't let the disapproval of others
destroy your life.*

My mother-in-law is an amazing woman. She's hard-working, committed to her children, generous with her grand-children, firm in her convictions, and energetic in her determination to make a positive difference in the lives of individuals who are physically or mentally challenged. Watching her get behind a cause and implement a plan is like watching a one-person army move a whole platoon into formation for the desired aim. She gets things done!

*"Lord, let me never enter a life,
except to build."*

—LILA TROTMAN, QUOTED FROM *A CHINA PLATE FOUND IN A GIFT SHOP*

At the age of seventeen she found herself pregnant and unmarried. On the day of that baby's birth, her own mother walked into the room, looked at the infant in her daughter's arms, and said, "For the last nine months I've prayed this child would be born dead."

When I heard this story, I felt weak in the knees and faint in my heart. You see, the baby my mother-in-law was holding in her arms that day is my husband. If Grandma had gotten her wish then, I would have missed out on marrying an incredible man. I'm able to tell the story now since Grandma has passed on. I know now that she was filled with the fear of facing her friends and family with the news of a child conceived out of wedlock.

Mom married the father of her child, and as time passed, Grandma did grow to love the grandchild she had earlier rejected.

Thinking about my mother-in-law's situation, I wondered how she was able to face her past and get on with her future in such a successful way. In spite of the initial disapproval from her own mother, she became confident, able to see the positive side of a negative life situation.

I have never wanted to pry into the details of all that transpired between my mother-in-law and Grandma during the days following Gene's birth, but I'm sure that Mom chose a constructive resolution for dealing with her early fears. You see, I've observed her making faith-filled decisions on a regular basis for many years — and that takes practice![1]

*God, make a fresh start in me,*
*shape a Genesis week from the chaos of my life.*
Psalm 51:10, MSG

152

# Five Words That Changed My Life

YVONNE HOWARD CHAPMAN

LIFE LESSON FROM MOTHER:
*When "the small stuff" gets you down,
remember "it's all small stuff" in the light
of eternity.*

In 1989 my husband and I were in a car accident that nearly took our lives. As my body began to heal, I realized the real challenge was living with the effects of my head injury. The changes in my personality, the accompanying emotional swings, and my negative outlook on life left me with a major attitude problem.

Trying to start life over again was difficult—no, *impossible.* And my greatest frustration always came from the little things. Tactless people. Physical struggles. Emotional battles. The frustration of needing more time to do simple tasks.

Just being in my mother's presence during those days had a calming effect on my emotions. She sensed my frustration and understood the depression and physical pain. When I allowed the little things to become big, she would smile and gently say, "Remember, *in the light of eternity . . .*"

With those five words, Mother taught me to develop an eternal perspective. The world would not fall apart if it took longer to perform a daily task. God didn't love me less because I wasn't as efficient as I was before the accident. My problems, which occasionally seemed like mountains, were little foothills in the light of what Christ did for me.

*"For people who are trapped in pain . . .
heaven promises a time far longer and
more substantial than the time we spent on
earth . . . The Bible never belittles human
disappointment . . . but it does add one key
word:* temporary. *What we feel now, we will
not always feel."*

—PHILIP YANCEY, *DISAPPOINTMENT WITH GOD*

Today I am healthy and whole, but I'm still learning a
lot about patience, and I still face an occasional mountain.
And every time I get frustrated, I hear Mom's soft voice
repeating the words that changed my life. "Remember, in
the light of eternity . . ."

*I don't think there's any comparison
between the present hard times
and the coming good times.
The created world itself can hardly wait
for what's coming next. Everything in creation
is being more or less held back. God reins it in until
both creation and all the creatures are ready
and can be released at the same moment
into the glorious times ahead.
Meanwhile, the joyful anticipation deepens.*
ROMANS 8:18-21, MSG

# Turning Fear Into Faith

KATHE WUNNENBERG

LIFE LESSON FROM MOTHER:
*Mothers who pass on their family's faith
stories give their children the gift of hope.*

I was not prepared to hear my doctor's words. I always believed things like this happened to other people, but not to me. I was wrong.

"You're pregnant," my doctor announced.

I was stunned. After fifteen years of marriage, years of infertility, and a wonderful adopted six-year-old son, I was pregnant! This was not part of my plan. Speaking, traveling, writing, and ministry were on my agenda for this season in my life—not a baby, diapers, and 2:00 A.M. feedings. But during the next few weeks, as my waistline disappeared, I slowly began to embrace the fact that I really was pregnant.

Reality hit on Good Friday when my husband, son, and I went to see our baby on the ultrasound. Tiny hands waved at us from the television screen. Although we were thrilled, I detected an uneasiness in the technician. When she abruptly left the room, I looked at my husband and said, "There's something wrong."

Moments later the technician returned with a doctor and my fears were confirmed. "I'm so sorry. Medical science has no conclusive answers why this condition occurs. Your baby is not developing properly." The doctor paused. "Your baby has no chance of survival."

Silence pervaded the room. The doctor mentioned termination of the pregnancy as an option, but at that moment, the baby kicked my ribs. "This baby is very much alive," I calmly replied. "We may not know *why* things happen, but we certainly know *who* controls the final outcome. We're going all the way with this pregnancy."

As we left the doctor's office for our preplanned celebration lunch, my young son Jake looked up at me with his penetrating brown eyes, "Mom, is our baby going to die?"

"Yes," I blurted out, and Jake erupted into tears.

I felt convicted in my spirit. Pausing, I looked at my son and spoke slowly, "Jake, I can't really say that, because I would be playing God. Although the doctors say the baby will die, only God knows what will really happen. We are going to trust His results and we'll be okay with whatever He decides."

Jake immediately responded with a confidence and faith that surprised me. "Okay, Mom!" he said.

The next several hours were grievous for us. Ironically, on this Easter weekend we found ourselves walking through our own Garden of Gethsemane, crying out, "Father, take this cup of suffering from us." We had a choice to make. Shake our fist at God, or run to Him and trust Him. In the midst of our pain that Easter weekend, we finally submitted our desires to His authority and said, "Not our will, but thine be done."

Even though I knew God was in control and I had committed to trust Him, I felt so alone. My heart ached with uncertainty. I was afraid. How could I endure this? I curled up on my sofa and pleaded with God to give me hope and courage. Sleepless, yet exhausted, I closed my eyes.

My thoughts drifted to a time several months earlier when my mom had flown in to surprise me for my birthday. While sipping flavored coffee in my backyard under a moonlit sky, we were enjoying our evening ritual of conversation. This particular evening was Mom's turn to do most of the talking.

"Kathe, God prompted me to come to see you. For some reason I believe you need encouragement. That's what I want to give you for your birthday—*words* to give you hope and courage."

I was surprised. I told Mom that everything was going great.

But she continued. "Kathe, you never know when you might need to remember what I'm going to tell you."

My ears tingled. I felt like some deep dark secret was about to be revealed.

Mom continued. "Your great-grandmother, Mother Young, was an awesome woman of God. She gave birth to twin boys prematurely in the early 1900s and no one expected them to live. But she never gave up. She asked God to intervene. And He did. One baby lived. He was your grandpa.

"Grandpa?" I gulped.

She nodded and continued. "Grandpa grew up and married a woman who had lost two infant sons. Doctors said she could never have another child. But she never gave up. She prayed and trusted God. He did the impossible and gave her three daughters. That was *my* mom—your Grannie!"

My amazement mounted as the story continued.

Mom recalled my birth story. She had tried for several years to have a second child and finally God allowed her to have me. Through tears Mom relived the details of almost losing me to a raging fever that lasted for days. Doctors told her that *if* I survived I would be brain-damaged.

"I never gave up hope, Kathe. Just remember that every time you smile in the mirror and see your gray-tinted teeth. The discoloration was caused by the medication given to you during that time. It's God's reminder to trust Him and always to have hope and courage, like those before you."

*"Faith is not the absence of fear or doubt, but the force that gets you safely through those long, dark, waiting-room hours."*

—M. WOMACH, *QUOTABLE QUOTES*

I opened my eyes and looked around my family room. It was 2:00 A.M. The baby within me kicked my ribs and I realized I wasn't dreaming. Although my mom was fifteen hundred miles away, I felt like she was sitting next to me.

God continued to use Mom's "faith stories" to give me hope and courage during the long months of waiting on the birth of my baby. I learned a whole *journey* of life lessons. On different days I laughed . . . cried . . . learned the necessity of silence and solitude . . . bonded with my unborn baby . . . released control . . . allowed others to encourage me . . . watched miracles happen and faith at work in others. I tasted humility and surrender, and I learned what it means to enjoy every moment. I learned how precious praying friends are, and I learned what mountain-moving faith really is, and how faithful and loving God is to care about me personally.

We planned a "praise celebration" for after the baby's birth, not knowing whether it would be a memorial or a dedication service. Our family prayed for a miracle, knowing that God would be glorified in an uncommon way through the birth of this child. We endeavored to persevere, press on, and trust God for the opportunity to touch lives for Jesus in the hospital and far beyond.

Although I didn't know what the future held for me and my baby, I was certain of *who* held the future. A mighty God. A God who can do all things. A God who hears our prayers. A God who knows just what we need. A God who gave me hope and courage through my mom's stories of faith.

A legacy I will pass on to the next generation.

Postscript: On August 22, John Samuel was born with eyes looking up at God. His birth was a celebration of God's love and a testimony of the value of every life. Within a few hours heaven's gates opened and welcomed John Samuel into the arms of Jesus. His brief life touched thousands of people with the reality of God, and the ripple effects will only be known in eternity. God *did* turn fear into confident faith.

*So, my son, throw yourself*
*into this work for Christ.*
*Pass on what you heard from me—*
*the whole congregation saying Amen!—*
*to reliable leaders who are competent*
*to teach others.*
2 Timothy 2:1-2, MSG

# My Tribute

To:_____

The Life Lesson You Taught Me Was:_____

_____

_____

_____

_____

_____

_____

My Favorite Memory of You Is:_____

_____

_____

_____

_____

_____

_____

_____

_____

_____

_____

_____

Signed_____

# Contributors

### Sandra P. Aldrich

Sandra P. Aldrich is a Kentucky storyteller. A prolific writer, some of Sandra's books include: *Living Through the Loss of Someone You Love, From One Single Mother to Another, Sheltered By the King,* and *Husbands Read Newspapers, Not Minds.* The former senior editor of *Focus on the Family* magazine and a popular guest on numerous radio and television shows, Sandra speaks and writes extensively on joyful living, marriage and family issues, and single parenting. For scheduling information, contact Alive Communications, Inc., 1465 Kelly Johnson Blvd., Suite 320, Colorado Springs, CO 80920. Phone: (719) 260-7080, Fax: (719) 260-8223.

### Julie Baker

Julie Baker is an accomplished songwriter and recording artist who travels nationally in concert ministry. Her uplifting CDs include *Attitude of Praise* and *Never Say Goodbye.* A former English teacher, Julie is currently an administrator at Cornerstone College in Grand Rapids, Michigan, where she works in media relations. She is also the coordinator of "Time Out—For Women Only" events. For concert booking information: (800) 937-6163.

### Dee Brestin

Dee Brestin is a national retreat speaker and best-selling author on women's relationships. Her books include *The Friendships of Women* and *We Are Sisters.* She has written her own line of Bible study guides for women (Victor) and has penned many of the Fisherman Bible study guides (Shaw Publishers). She can be contacted through Shaw Publishers (1-800-SHAW-PUB) or at 11 Lakeview Drive, Kearney, NE 68847. Phone: (308) 237-7611.

### Jan Carlberg

Jan Carlberg is a second-generation Baptist preacher's kid who loves telling the stories of Jesus in person or on paper. She is married to Judson Carlberg, president of Gordon College in Wenham, Massachusetts. She is also the proud mother of two grown children, Heather and Chad. For scheduling information, contact Jan c/o Gordon College, 255 Grapevine Road, Wenham, MA 01984. Phone: (508) 927-2306, Ext. 4202; Fax: (508) 524-3700.

### Yvonne Howard Chapman

Yvonne Howard Chapman is a talented Christian concert artist and speaker. She and her husband, Jerry, travel extensively in ministry, sharing their dynamic testimony of God's faithfulness through the months and years of healing following a car accident that nearly took their lives. For concert and conference information, contact Yvonne at P. O. Box 61198, Columbia, SC 29260. Phone: (803) 782-6515.

### Anne Denmark

Anne Denmark is a self-proclaimed "pack rat with a purpose." Her true passion is using her creative gift of encouragement through teaching, parenting three teenagers, and being a "freelance servant of God." A former director of Christian education, Anne trains speakers and Bible teachers in creative teaching techniques as an instructor at "Speak Up With Confidence" seminars through Carol Kent Ministries. Married to a family physician, Anne and her husband are active volunteers in mission projects around the world. For information, contact Anne at 1132 S.W. Heritage Dr., El Reno, OK 73036. Phone: (405) 262-9412.

### Jennie Afman Dimkoff

Jennie Afman Dimkoff is a Christian motivational speaker and businesswoman who travels widely in ministry throughout the U.S. and Canada. A member of the National Speakers Association, Jennie assists her sister, Carol Kent, as a team teacher in the "Speak Up With Confidence" seminar. She is the founder and director of Story Line Ministries and is the storyteller for Kids'

Time Story Line. For scheduling information, contact Jennie at 338 E. Main Street, Fremont, MI 49412. Phone: (616) 924-0015, Fax: (616) 924-6611.

### Sherrie Eldridge

Sherrie Eldridge is a freelance writer and speaker living in Indianapolis, Indiana. In addition to being a wife, mother, and grandmother of twins, she is the founder of Jewel Among Jewels Adoption Network, Inc. She welcomes feedback at P. O. Box 502065, Indianapolis, IN 46250.

### Cynthia Fantasia

Cynthia Fantasia is on the pastoral staff at Grace Chapel in Lexington, Massachusetts, as director of women's ministries. With a ministry focus on the transforming love of Jesus and development of women, Cynthia is active in speaking, teaching, and counseling. She oversees weekly programs that reach several hundred women, and mentors emerging women's ministry leaders across the country. For information, contact Cynthia at Grace Chapel, 3 Militia Drive, Lexington, MA 02173. Phone: (617) 862-6499, Fax: (617) 674-2824.

### Mary Farrar

Mary Farrar is the author of the popular book, *Choices: For Women Who Long to Discover Life's Best.* Mary has been teaching women for twenty-five years, and occasionally speaks at marriage conferences with her husband, Dr. Steve Farrar. Steve has a national conference ministry to men and is author of the best-seller, *Point Man.* The Farrars live in Dallas, Texas, with their three teenage children, and can be reached through Men's Leadership, Inc., 3000 Briarcrest Drive, Suite 312, Bryan, TX 77802, or by calling 1 (800) MEN-LEAD.

### Barbi Franklin

Barbi Franklin grew up singing in her family's music ministry. As part of The Murk Family Singers she traveled extensively around the world. Today Barbi is married to Terry Franklin. Together, as

Dove Award-winning songwriters and recording artists, they travel internationally in music ministry. Their concert ministry theme is: "Inspiring Love in the Home and Revival in the Church." For concert information, contact Terry & Barbi Franklin at P.O. Box 17164, Nashville, TN 37217. Phone: (615) 360-6104, Fax: (615) 360-7352, or E-mail: internet:family@edge.net.

### Becky Freeman

Becky Freeman lives in the boonies of East Texas with her patient husband, Scott, and her four children. Becky and her mother Ruthie, coauthored the best-seller *Worms in My Tea & Other Mixed Blessings* (a Gold Medallion Finalist) and *Adult Children of Fairly Functional Parents*. Becky's latest "solo" books are *Marriage 9-1-1* and *Still Lickin' the Spoon & Other Confessions of a Grown-up Kid*. Becky is a frequent guest on radio and television and writes a monthly "Marriage 911" column for *Home Life Magazine*. For information, contact Becky at Rt. 5, Box 229 H, Greenville, TX 75402. Phone/Fax: (903) 883-4512.

### Jeannette Clift George

Jeannette Clift George is the founder and artistic director of the A.D. Players, the Houston-based Christian Theater Company which offers plays throughout the world. She has extensive background in professional theater, including acting off-Broadway and touring with the New York Shakespeare Company. She was nominated for a Golden Globe Award for her portrayal of Corrie ten Boom in the film, *The Hiding Place*. Jeannette is the author of two books, *Some Run with Feet of Clay* and *Travel Tips from a Reluctant Traveler*. She has written numerous plays which are now available through Lillenas Publishing's new A.D. Players Series. For information, contact Jeannette at A.D. Players, 2710 West Alabama, Houston, TX 77098. Phone: (713) 528-0481.

### Dr. Judy Briscoe Golz

Dr. Judy Briscoe Golz was born in England, the only girl of Stuart and Jill Briscoe's three children. She has a Ph.D. in community psychology and is a visiting instructor in the Department of

Pastoral Counseling and Psychology at Trinity Evangelical Divinity School. She has coauthored three books with her mother. She is married to Greg and they have three sons. The Golz family lives in River Forest, Illinois.

### Nancy Groom

Nancy Groom holds a degree in education from Calvin College and has taught English and Bible. Her first book, *Married Without Masks,* was published in 1989, later to be followed by *From Bondage to Bonding,* and, most recently, *Heart to Heart About Men.* In addition to a busy writing schedule, Nancy speaks at many conferences and retreats all over the United States. In her spare time, Nancy and her husband, Bill, enjoy riding their Harley-Davidson motorcycle. They reside in Miami, Florida.

### Dr. Karen Johnson Hayter

Dr. Karen Johnson Hayter is the producer and host of COPE, a daily nationwide, live television call-in program that is aired on Odyssey and FamilyNet. She is a licensed, professional therapist and has contributed articles to numerous periodicals. Karen is also a contributor to the Woman's Study Bible, published by Thomas Nelson in 1995. For information, contact Karen at COPE, 6350 West Freeway, Fort Worth, TX 76150. Phone: (800) 292-2287, Fax: (817) 735-1790.

### Cynthia Heald

Cynthia Heald is a native Texan. She and her husband, Jack, a veterinarian by profession, are on full-time staff with The Navigators in Tucson, Arizona. They have four children and five grandchildren. Cynthia graduated from the University of Texas with a degree in English. She is the author of the best-selling NavPress Bible studies: *Becoming a Woman of Excellence, Becoming a Woman of Freedom, Becoming a Woman of Purpose,* and *Becoming a Woman of Prayer.*

### Daisy Hepburn

Daisy Hepburn is a writer and speaker who shares motivational and encouraging ideas with women across the country. Her dynamic style is known to captivate audiences at a variety of conventions and retreats throughout the year. Her books include *Forget Not His Blessings, How to Grow a Women's Minis-tree,* and *What's So Glorious about Everyday Living?* Daisy is currently Minister to Women at Scottsdale Bible Church. For information, contact Daisy at the church at 7601 E. Shea Blvd., Scottsdale, AZ 85260. Phone: (602) 984-7810, Fax: (602) 948-2679.

### Liz Curtis Higgs

Liz Curtis Higgs is the author of six books, including *Only Angels Can Wing It* and *"One Size Fits All" and Other Fables* (Thomas Nelson). She is a columnist for *Today's Christian Woman* and has written humorous articles for *Marriage Partnership* and *Home Life.* A busy retreat and conference speaker, Liz lives in Louisville, Kentucky, with her husband, Bill, and two children, Matthew and Lillian. For information, contact Liz at P. O. Box 43577, Louisville, KY 40253-0577. Phone: (502) 254-5454, E-mail: internet:LizHiggs@aol.com.

### Cynthia Spell Humbert

Cynthia Spell Humbert is a popular retreat and seminar speaker. A Christian counselor specializing in women's issues, Cynthia's background includes counseling at the Minirth-Meier Clinic in Richardson, Texas, where she was frequently featured on the clinic's nationally syndicated radio program. Cynthia is also a freelance writer and has contributed to a number of Minirth-Meier books. For scheduling information, contact Cynthia at 7602 Oneida Ct., Wichita, KS 67206. Phone: (316) 634-6843.

### Luan Zemmer Jackson, MS, RN

Luan Jackson is a "people builder," and has been conducting seminars for over ten years. Her ministry has taken her around the world to China, Bangladesh, Venezuela, and England. She is a member of the National Speakers Association and has a master's degree in biological behavioral nursing. Luan owns and operates a full service mental health clinic. For booking information, call (810) 664-4641, Fax: (810) 667-4488.

### Margaret Jensen

Margaret Jensen is an extraordinary storyteller, writer, speaker, and grandmother. Her eleven books include the best-selling *First We Have Coffee* and *Lena*. Margaret's short stories have been published in a wide variety of Christian magazines. She travels extensively throughout the United States, Canada, and Europe, reminding people that they need a personal encounter with Jesus Christ. For information, write Margaret at 229 Oakleaf Drive, Wilimington, NC 29403.

### Dee Jepsen

Dee Jepsen is National President of Enough Is Enough, a non-profit organization that educates, mobilizes, and equips Americans in the battle against pornography. Dee is married to former U.S. Senator Roger Jepsen, and she served under President Reagan on the President's Task Force on Private Sector Initiatives, and as a special assistant to the president as liaison between women's organizations and the White House. An award-winning author, Dee is also a national and international lecturer and serves on the board or special project committees of fifteen different organizations. For information, write Enough Is Enough, P. O. Box 888, Fairfax, VA 22030. Phone: (703) 278-8343, Fax: (703) 278-8510.

### Carol John

Carol John travels internationally, speaking to groups in schools, churches, and businesses, using the stories of her life to share the good news of the sovereignty and goodness of God. She has a master's degree in cell biology and has taught biology in community colleges. Carol programmed computers for eighteen years before beginning a speaking career. She is single and lives with her mother, a widow, in Oxnard, California. For scheduling information, contact Carol John at (800) 350-4886, Fax: (805) 983-8170.

### Carolyn Lunn

Carolyn Lunn is a gifted speaker and Bible study teacher. The author of *Joy Anyway!*, Carolyn is also a contributor to numerous curriculum studies and has been published in many periodicals. She is married to Vernon Lunn and has three adult children and four grandchildren. For scheduling information, contact Carolyn at 13627 Sycamore, Olathe, KS 66062. Phone: (913) 780-5866.

### Nell Maxwell

Nell Maxwell is the founder and president of Women Alive, the largest interdenominational ministry for women in Canada. Women Alive began twenty-four years ago. Today conferences are held in many provinces each year, along with Bible studies, evangelistic outreaches, and a national publication called *The Branch*. A registered nurse, Nell is also an author, conference speaker, wife, mother, and grandmother. For information, contact Nell c/o Women Alive, 30 Mary St., Barrie, Ontario L4N 1S8, Canada. Phone: (705) 726-3803, Fax: (705) 726-8439.

### Carole Mayhall

Carole Mayhall and her husband, Jack, live in Colorado Springs and have worked with The Navigators since 1956. They currently minister with The Navigators in the field of marriage and the family, giving seminars in the United States and overseas. Carole has written seven books and cowritten two others with Jack. She also speaks frequently at women's retreats. For scheduling information, contact Carole at 5720 Velvet Court, Colorado Springs, CO 80918. Phone: (719) 534-9999, Fax: (719) 534-9490.

### Dottie McDowell

Dottie McDowell is the mother of four children: Sean and Kelly are in college; Katie is attending high school, and Heather is in elementary school. She is the coauthor of four children's books and is the wife of Josh McDowell, traveling speaker and author with Campus Crusade for Christ. Dottie assists Josh in editing his materials and works with him on special projects.

### Lucinda Secrest McDowell

"Cindy" Secrest McDowell has been writing and talking all of her life—but now that she's a grown-up, she's known as an author and conference speaker! She celebrated her fortieth birthday by writing two books: *Amazed by Grace* and *Women's Spiritual Passages: Celebrating Faith After 40!* She is married and the mother of four children. Cindy has been published in more than fifty magazines and was named 1993 "Writer of the Year" at the Mt. Hermon Writers Conference. For scheduling information, write to: Encouraging Words! Box 290707, Wethersfield, CT 06129. Phone: (860) 529-7175, Fax: (860) 721-7861.

### Laurie McIntyre

Laurie McIntyre is enjoying her eighth year as pastor of women's ministries at Elmbrook Church in Brookfield, Wisconsin, a ministry that draws over one thousand women weekly. A vibrant conference, retreat, and seminar speaker, Laurie is also coauthor with Jill Briscoe of *Designing Effective Women's Ministries*. For scheduling information, contact Laurie at 777 South Barker Road, Brookfield, WI 53045. Phone: (414) 786-7051, Fax: (414) 796-5752.

### Kathy Collard Miller

Kathy Collard Miller is a wife, mother, speaker, and author. She is the best-selling author of the *God's Vitamin "C" for the Spirit* series and twenty-five other books, including the *Daughters of the King Bible Study Series*. Her articles have appeared in numerous periodicals and she is frequently interviewed on television and radio programs. For scheduling information, contact Kathy at P. O. Box 1058, Placentia, CA 92871. Phone: (714) 993-2654, Fax: (714) 993-1833, E-mail: internet:Kathyspeak@aol.com.

### Lindsey O'Connor

Lindsey O'Connor is a wife and mother of four, author, speaker, and broadcaster (just never all at once!). She's the author of

*If Mama Ain't Happy, Ain't Nobody Happy* and *Working at Home*. She has worked on both sides of the microphone, as guest or broadcaster on programs including, "Focus on the Family" and "Point of View." Lindsey speaks at conferences and to women's groups. Contact Lindsey at P. O. Box 9293, The Woodlands, TX 77387.

### Sandy Petro

Sandy Petro is a dynamic speaker and author of three books. As a certified personal trainer and owner of a fitness business, Sandy works one-on-one with women, helping them to achieve physical health and self-acceptance as they move toward spiritual maturity. For information, contact Sandy at FIRM, FIT, and FREE, 710 Executive Park Dr., Greenwood, IN 46143. Phone: (317) 889-0711, Fax: (317) 865-8176.

### Nellie Pickard

Nellie Pickard is a wife, mother of three, author, and speaker who addresses the topic of evangelism with "hands-on" passion. She has written four books, including *What Do You Say When?*, *What Would You Have Said?*, *Just Say It*, and her latest, *52 True Stories of Effective Witnessing*. For information, contact Nellie at 23910 Trailwood Ct., Bingham Farms, MI 48025. Phone: (810) 644-0943.

### Naomi Rhode

Naomi Rhode is an accomplished professional speaker who has shared her expertise as a communications consultant with audiences in all fifty states and thirteen countries around the globe. A former president of the National Speakers Association and current member of the Board of Directors for NSA, she was one of the first women in North America to be honored with the coveted Council of Peers Award of Excellence (CPAE) from the organization. Naomi is the author of two inspirational books, *The Gift of Family—A Legacy of Love* and *More Beautiful Than Diamonds—The Gift of Friendship*. For information, contact SmartPractice, 3400 East McDowell, Phoenix, AZ 85008. Phone: (602) 225-9090, Fax: (602) 225-0599.

### Valerie Elliot Shepard

Valerie Elliot Shepard is the only daughter of Elisabeth and Jim Elliot. Valerie, less than one year old when her missionary father was killed by Auca Indians, spent the first eight years of her childhood in Ecuador. She now stays busy as a home-school teacher, pastor's wife, and mother of eight children. Her husband, Walt Shepard, Jr., pastors Aliso Creek Presbyterian Church in Laguna Niguel, California.

### Betty Southard

Betty Southard is a popular international speaker, Bible teacher, and author of *The Grandmother Book*. She is the minister of caring for a large television ministry and serves on the Board of Directors of Royal Family Kid's Camps, Christian Women's International Network, and the International Women's Conference. She is also on the teaching staff of Christian Leaders, Authors, and Speakers Seminars (CLASS). For booking information, contact CLASS Speakers at (800) 433-6633.

### Carol Travilla

Carol Travilla is a pastor's wife, seminar leader, and author of *Caring Without Wearing* (NavPress). A former psychologist and marriage and family therapist, Carol specializes in helping women to integrate their faith, family, and career through a Life-Plan process. Her life passion is working one-to-one with women who desire to be all that God designed them to be. For information, write Carol at 4143 W. Bart Drive, Chandler, AZ 85226. Phone: (602) 940-4542, Fax: (602) 940-1976.

### Kathe Wunnenberg

Kathe Wunnenberg is a speaker, writer, leader, and encourager. She is the Executive Director of Christian Business Women's Association, a ministry committed to equipping and encouraging professional women to live their faith in the workplace. Kathe's articles are published monthly in the *Faith at Work* newsletter. For information, contact Kathe at 4609 E. McNeil Street, Phoenix, AZ 85044. Phone: (602) 893-2386, Fax: (602) 496-6534.

# A Postscript

This morning I was reminded of why I compiled the life lessons in this book. I spoke at a brunch for "MOPS" (Mothers of Preschoolers) and the women I met could provide enough material for a second volume of vignettes on the triumphs and tears of being a mom! They swapped stories about everything mothers need to discuss with each other: personal fears, childhood diseases, discipline problems, fatigue and time pressures, marital challenges, and practical solutions for coping with daily life.

One mom told about her son's recent illness:

> When Michael was almost three years old, he became very sick in the middle of the night and vomited several times. After the first episode, I gave him a dishpan to have at his bedside. Before leaving the room, I gave careful instructions. "Honey, put your head in the bucket the next time you feel sick."
>
> An hour later he was throwing up again and I heard him calling for me. Rushing into Michael's bedroom, I found him flat on his back, arms at his side, with the dish pan *over his head*! There was vomit nestled in his ears, matted in his hair, trickling down his neck, and covering his pajamas.
>
> I suddenly realized my child had done *exactly* what I told him to do: "Put your head *in the bucket* the next time you feel sick."
>
> Obviously, I hadn't explained the procedure properly![1]

We not only learn life lessons from our mothers; we learn them from our children, too! As I watched these women laugh and cry together, I realized how much we need each other. I hope the stories in this book inspired you. But more than that, I pray that you have been challenged to practice biblical principles for raising your own children.

By the way, if you have a humorous or inspiring story to tell about one of your children, send it my way. This book may need a follow-up on *life lessons we've learned from our kids*!

Send stories and inquiries to:

Carol Kent Ministries
P. O. Box 610941
Port Huron, MI 48061-0941
Phone: (810) 982-0898
Fax: (810) 987-4163

# Notes

### The Pixie Dust Extravaganza
1. "The Pixie Dust Extravaganza" as adapted from "Dream" in the *Mom's Check-Up*, Dottie McDowell and Dave Ray, © 1994. Core Ministries Royal Oak, MI. All rights reserved. Used by permission.

### An Ugly, Old, Beautiful Woman
1. Adapted excerpt from *Worms in My Tea and Other Mixed Blessings* by Becky Freeman and Ruthie Arnold, © 1994. Used by permission, Broadman & Holman Publishers.

### A Snapshot of Elisabeth Elliot
1. Adapted from an article that originally appeared in *Christian Parenting*. Used by permission of Valerie Elliot Shepard.

### A Snapshot of Jill Briscoe
1. Adapted from an article that originally appeared in *Christian Parenting*. Used by permission of Dr. Judy Briscoe Golz.

### My Mother's Songs
1. Psalm 27:1
2. Often people who are born with a chemical imbalance do not know it until they experience their first severe stress. I share this, and Sally does as well, because we believe many Christians do not understand this. While they would never tell a diabetic to forego his insulin and just trust God, they *do* give that kind of advice to people who suffer from a chemical imbalance and are experiencing depression.

### The Harmonica Lady
1. Daisy Hepburn, *Forget Not His Blessings* (Nashville: Thomas Nelson Publishers, 1993), adapted from pp. 154-156. Used by permission.

### A Cruel Remark
1. Carol Kent, *Tame Your Fears* (Colorado Springs: NavPress, 1993), adapted from pp. 138-140. Used by permission.

### A Postscript
1. Used by permission of Pat Spreng.

# Author

CAROL KENT is the founder and president of "Speak Up With Confidence" seminars, a ministry committed to helping Christians develop their communication skills.

A member of the National Speakers Association, Carol is scheduled more than a year in advance to speak at conferences and retreats throughout the United States and Canada. She is also a frequent guest on a wide variety of radio and television broadcasts, including "Focus on the Family," "Prime Time America," "Chapel of the Air," and "100 Huntley Street."

Carol has a B.S. degree in speech education and an M.A. in communication arts from Western Michigan University. Her background includes four years as a drama, speech, and English teacher, and two years as director of the Alternative Education Program for pregnant teenagers. After a brief time of working as a director of women's ministries at a midwestern church, she went into full-time speaking.

Carol's other books include *Secret Longings of the Heart, Tame Your Fears, Speak Up With Confidence,* and *Detours, Tow Trucks, and Angels in Disguise* (all NavPress).

Carol and her husband, Gene, live in Port Huron, Michigan. They have one son, Jason, who is currently a student at the United States Naval Academy. They also have a temperamental Himalayan cat named Bahgi.